Teach Yourself to Swim . . .
Despite Your Fear of Water

Teach Yourself to Swim . . . Despite Your Fear of Water

Mick Arellano

*Illustrations by Kirk Lyttle,
Marilyn Wick, and Mick Arellano*

HAWTHORN BOOKS, INC.
Publishers / NEW YORK
A Howard & Wyndham Company

Library of Congress Catalog Card Number: 77-90092
ISBN: 0-8015-7462-5

1 2 3 4 5 6 7 8 9 10

Contents

Preface

This book is dedicated to all of you who are afraid of water but would like to learn to swim. Here is a method of instruction that can teach you to become a swimmer.

For many years I myself was afraid of water, so I am aware of the problems you face as a fearful nonswimmer. I know, for example, how it feels to see water as an enemy and what it means to be terrified by the very thought of going into water. I know how it feels to want to swim even though you are afraid to try. I understand your desperation and frustration, because I once had that same experience.

But I also know that the greatest problem you face is that there is no place to turn for help. You are stuck with your fear of water because proper assistance is not available to you. There are, for example, virtually no beginning swimming courses pertinent to your special needs. And in spite of all the swimming books available at stores and libraries, very few books are even slightly useful to people who fear water.

This book, then, was written because there should be a beginning swimming program for people who are afraid of water; it was written because *you* should have a chance to learn to swim. This is not a manual for instructors or regular beginning swimmers. It is a self-help book intended exclusively for fearful nonswimmers like you. This is a personal handbook that provides you with specialized and practical swimming instruction. It is the workable system I invented to teach myself and others to swim, and it will show you, too, how to become a swimmer.

Introduction

Many people experience too much water too soon. It is not an uncommon occurrence. Neither is it uncommon for such people to develop a peculiar dread of water. This is the case in the following tale of woe. Our character is a victim of terrible circumstances, and the situation—both bleak and funny—is familiar to many of us.

You're eight years old and it's a terrific summer afternoon. The sun is hot, the sky is big and blue.

A car pulls up. It's your aunt and two cousins. Would you like to picnic at the lake with us? Hey, yeah!

The lake is not far, but the drive seems to take forever. Your cousins are great pals, and everyone in the back seat is very excited. Who has the lotion? Stop poking me! Aren't we there yet?

Down the beach you run. Yikes, you should have worn shoes. The sand is practically on fire, and your aunt is already yelling at you. Don't run so fast! Don't kick sand on anybody! Don't step on that baby! You dump everything onto the crumpled blanket and head for the water.

Ah, the cool liquid feels so good on your scorched feet. Just take a few seconds to wiggle those toes before you gallop into deeper water. Your cousins are already in water up to their chests, and you join in the splash war.

Further out you go, beyond your cousins. Up to your shoulders and the water feels fine. You look back at your cousins and wave happily.

You look for your aunt . . . but you can't see her. You can't even see the beach. The bottom has dropped from under you, and all you see is water. Lots of water. You breathe the stuff, it's all around you. Your chest begins to feel heavy. Then suddenly, somehow, darkness washes over you.

Six years later to the day you are standing in a huge, dank, cement room with twenty other people. There are no windows, and the whole room is thick with the stench of chlorine and sweat. Everyone is mulling around in same-color swimming suits, laughing and jostling. But you're not in the least amused. Did Jonah laugh when he was trapped in the gut of a whale?

In the center of the room lies a grey, deep pool. Very, very deep. The water sloshes against the pool's edge like a giant, lapping mouth. And you can't seem to take your eyes off it.

"Over here," someone yells. It's the instructor. "Everyone over here by the blackboard. I need your name and swimming experience."

The class moves toward the blackboard, but you hesitate and glance back at the pool. You can smell the chlorine. You can hear the water waiting for you.

"Swum before?" says the instructor, motioning to you.

"It stinks in here . . . " you mutter.

"Have you ever had lessons before, or are you a beginner?"

"I'm a beginner," you say.

"You've never swum before?" demands the instructor.

"No . . . not exactly." The class stares at you. "Well . . . a little."

That is Monday.

On Friday you find yourself sitting on the edge of the pool, your feet dangling into the water. Most of the class have already swum the length of the pool. And you know you will be called next. You can feel it.

"Okay, let me see here—"says the instructor, as you sit there squirming and fidgeting and sweating and wishing you could disappear.

They've been dropping in alphabetical order, and you've got to be next. So what's all this lousy suspense! Besides, if they can do it, you can do it. Or so you try to tell yourself as the instructor shuffles through his notes.

"You there, you're next. Get ready to dive into the pool and swim to the other end."

It surprises you when you stand up. You know you can't swim two feet. You've been faking it all week long. Most of your energy, in fact, has been spent figuring ways to *avoid* the swimming exercises. Yet here you are preparing to take on the entire stinking pool. The best thing for you to do is to march out of there and go home. You realize this. But just the same you stand there, hovering over the pool.

"Whenever you're ready," says the instructor.

And blindly, for some crazy unknown reason, you lean your body forward. You flop into the water, and lie there like a dead fish. Only you don't float. You sink.

"Move your arms and legs! You've got to move your arms and legs!" screams the instructor as you bob back to the surface.

So you stab at the deep water. You bite it, kick it, swallow it, and vanish from the surface again. You reach desperately for something solid to grab onto. You pray to every god you've ever heard of, but all you find is water.

"It's impossible," you yell inside your head. "I can't do any of this lousy stuff. My legs are tired, they feel like cement. And the water is too deep. I can't reach anything."

"Move those arms and legs!" echoes faintly through the water. But the words miss their mark.

You remember that day with your aunt. Now you can see her: standing on the shore, signaling and shouting frantically. You want to smile and be free of this water, but the bottom has dropped from under you. Your chest begins to feel heavy. Then suddenly, somehow, darkness washes over you.

Teach Yourself to Swim . . .
Despite Your Fear of Water

1
What Is Fear of Water?

Fear of water is a learned fear. It is not a fear you were born with. It is the result of traumatic water experiences during your childhood or early adolescence. Your fear of water could have been caused by a near-drowning incident, a frightening boat ride, or even something as obscure as hearing a loud noise when you were first introduced to water as an infant. It is also possible that as a child you simply learned your fear of water from parents who were themselves afraid of water. There are several possible causes, but the question you should ask is: Once I became afraid of water, why did I stay that way? Why didn't I lose my fear of water? Why am I still afraid?

The answer is that fear of water is more than a learned fear. It is a learned fear that can be intensified if it isn't handled carefully and quickly. And it doesn't go away by itself. Like many other learned fears, the longer it persists the more it grows. And the more it grows, the more difficult it becomes to resolve.

However, even extreme fear of water can be resolved. It can be *un*learned. But this unlearning process can only occur if the fearful person is presented with many pleasant and nonfrightening water experiences. Unfortunately, after people do become afraid of water they seldom encounter anything that even faintly resembles a pleasant water experience. What they encounter instead are very unpleasant situations, which tend to intensify their fear of water.

Take your own case, for example. Your friends may have thoughtlessly harassed you at the beach. Your parents, through some misguided wisdom, may have forced you into the water, thinking that would help. Or you yourself may have decided to take a conventional beginning swimming class in the hope that the swimming instructor could solve your fear for you. But the instructor may not even have recognized your fear of water. Instead of being sensitive to your fear of water, he may have aggravated it severely and made it worse than it was before.

Most attempts at unlearning fear of water fail badly because most people—including swimming instructors—do not understand the true nature of the fear. Swimming instructors and psychologists propound the dos and don'ts of swimming instruction, but most of these experts have not themselves experienced fear of water. On the whole, therefore, they tend to overlook the problem. Or worse, they may spread misconceptions about fear of water that bear the stamp of authority.

Fear of water should not, for example, be confused with timidity or simple anxiety. Timidity, like shyness, is a general fear and is usually not intense. Anxiety is also a general fear—especially the fear of the unknown. Yet most swimming instructors and authors of beginning swimming books make just that mistake—they confuse the timid or anxious learner with fearful nonswimmers like you who have a particular and intense fear. Consequently, they try to dissolve your fear of water by simply appealing to your rationality or pride. But explanations of the physical laws of motion in water or repetition of the "nothing to fear but fear itself" incantation do not help you. These instructors are steering a false course. Fearful nonswimmers are not like other people. They are in a class by themselves, and they can't be talked out of their fear.

As a former fearful nonswimmer, it is clear to me that most swimming instructors have little understanding of what it means to be afraid of water. They do not recognize fear of water as a problem in itself and therefore cannot provide a solution to the problem. They have no sense of the very specific and intense terror that often grips a fearful nonswimmer when he encounters water, and they know little about the fearful nonswimmer himself.

The nonswimmer afraid of water is not a timid person by nature. In fact, studies have shown that with the exception of fear of water, most fearful nonswimmers are very well adjusted socially and have even more than the average will to achieve.* And the fear that fearful nonswimmers experience is definitely not a fear of the unknown. Quite the contrary. All fearful nonswimmers share exactly the same fear, and they know precisely what they are afraid of — *water!*

What Are You Really Afraid Of?

Okay. So we know something about the nature of your fear of water. It is an irrational fear that can afflict anyone. When triggered, it can be a terrifying, debilitating fear that floods the mind and extinguishes logic. It is a fear that can completely overwhelm even the most level-headed people.

But what is it about water that makes you fear it? It is surely not just water itself. You don't mind drinking water out of a glass, do you? And you don't mind washing your face or taking a bath. What, then, are the components of your fear of water? Let's try to analyze your fear and see exactly what it is you are afraid of.

Your fear of water is first of all a fear of *large bodies* of water. You are not afraid in the bathtub, for example, because in the tub you are a very big fish in a very little pond. There is no chance of anything going wrong. You are in complete control, and you feel secure. But in a large body of water, such as a swimming pool or lake, anything can happen to you — or so you think, anyway. You are no longer in control. You become a very little fish in a very large pond, and if something does go wrong, there is nothing you can do about it because you don't know how to swim.

*In one study to determine if different personality traits were in any way related to fear of water, it was found that the common assumption that fearful nonswimmers are generally timid people was not fact. Fearful nonswimmers and fearful swimmers (they exist, too) rated high in general confidence and resistance to fear. The researcher's conclusion was that fear of water is a different type of fear, which has no relation to general fearfulness. *Cecilia Trujillo, "Effects of Beginning Swimming Instruction on Selected Personality Traits," master's thesis, University of Washington, 1969, GV 361 — th 17767.*

Your fear of large bodies of water, then, is more specifically a fear of being helpless in large bodies of water. It is a fear of not knowing what to do if something goes wrong. You fear the loss of security. The only way to feel secure when you are in large bodies of water is to know how to swim—but you don't know how to swim.

So why can't you swim? Because you are afraid to try, you say, or you have already tried before and it frightened you. But what really frightens you about learning to swim? Not the thought of swimming itself, because you know that if you could swim you would feel secure. And not just water itself, because we have learned that under certain conditions you are not afraid of water. Why, then, won't you try to swim? What is it that really frightens you? The answer is that there are smaller, cumulative fears that cause your fear of water, and it is these specific fears that prevent you from becoming a swimmer.

You may, for example, be particularly afraid of getting water up your nose. Who isn't? It's painful and frightening. If water gets up your nose, you can't breathe—you gag and choke. You may also fear choking. You don't like to choke, even at the dinner table—it frightens you, you can't get any air. And if you happen to be in a large body of water when you choke, you may drown. Fear of drowning is, of course, the most obvious characteristic of anyone's fear of water, but behind that larger, more general fear lie the real culprits: your specific fears. And fear of choking, fear of getting water up your nose, and fear of loss of breath are just three of them.

What other specific fears may you have that prevent you from learning to swim? Well, you probably have a dreadful fear of loss of eyesight. You don't like the idea of not being able to see—especially in water, where you already feel insecure. But at the same time you may also have a fear of opening your eyes in water. So you may have two distinct eye-related fears.

You may also have a fear of sinking, a fear of loss of balance while standing in deep water, and a fear that you would be unable to recover from a loss of balance. And you may have a terrific fear of losing contact with terra firma. There is a need for you to cling to something solid. You don't like to lose contact with solid ground, or to reach for something to hang onto but find only water. Thus, as a consequence of these last four specific fears, you are afraid of deeper water.

There are some less common specific fears that can contribute to a person's fear of water. You may have a fear of heights and a fear of falling, for example, and it is not difficult to see how these fears could intensify your fears of sinking and loss of balance in water. There are also some subtle fears that may contribute to your fear of water. Fear that people will harass you if they suspect you are afraid of water can intensify your fear. It can even make your fear of water permanent, because you may be inclined not even to try to overcome your fear of water. And you can make your fear of water worse by trying to hide it. You should know that the more you repress your fear—*the more you fear your own fear*—the worse it becomes.

As a fearful nonswimmer, you may possess any or all of the above specific fears; you may also have other contributing fears which I have not mentioned. The result is your general fear of water. It is the combination of these specific fears that creates serious learning problems for you, problems serious enough to prevent you from trying to learn to swim in the conventional manner.

2
The Technique of Fear Avoidance

This handbook will work for you because you will learn to swim without encountering the full force of your fear of water. I will show you how to work around *the specific fears* that contribute to your overall fear. Your learning experience will be natural, nonfrightening, and secure. Every effort will be made to exclude potential panic situations from your learning program. You will finally have a real opportunity to learn to swim.

"Impossible," you might say. "The only way I could avoid fear of water would be to avoid water all together!" But that is where you are wrong. There are ways to avoid the experience of fear even when you are in the water, because *there are ways to work around your specific water-related fears*. And it is those specific fears, don't forget, that make up your general fear of water.

Remember, this is not a conventional method of swimming instruction. You and I are not bound to the rigid structure of a formal training class. When I say that you can avoid the experience of fear by working around your specific water-related fears, I am not deceiving you. I mean what I say, because we can afford to be imaginative—we must be imaginative, or you may never learn to swim. So since you, the fearful nonswimmer, would like nothing better than to be able to avoid the experience of fear by any means possible, that is exactly what we will do. We will

have you avoid the experience of fear by any means possible!
But we will accomplish that *in the water.*

The actual technique for avoiding fear is really quite simple.
We will merely work around the sources of your specific fears.
If, for example, you find you have a specific fear of deep water
(and most fearful nonswimmers naturally do) there will be a simple common sense solution to that problem: *Don't go into deep
water!* The source of that specific fear is the deep water itself,
and deep water is very avoidable, so avoid the source entirely.
There is no reason why this particular fear should prevent you
from learning to swim. You can learn to swim in shallow water.
That, in fact, is one of the main points of my teaching method:
fearful learners should learn to swim in shallow water.

Other specific fears, however, will be avoided in a slightly different way. Instead of avoiding the source of the fear entirely,
we will merely make a technical adjustment. If, for example,
you are afraid to open your eyes when your head is under water,
you should try wearing goggles. You will not be able to avoid the
necessity of opening your eyes underwater, but you will be able
to avoid the fear itself. You will make the task nonfearful by
using the artificial aid of a pair of goggles.

These other fear-avoidance techniques are blended into the
swimming instructions themselves. Many of them are simple to
perform; some are more challenging. All of the fear-avoidance
techniques, however, are well thought out and sensitive to your
particular needs. The important thing is for you to be open to
my suggestions. Remember, this method of fear avoidance has
worked—for me and for many other fearful nonswimmers. So
give these avoidance techniques a chance to work for you. Give
yourself a chance to avoid your specific fears and learn to swim.

Teach Yourself

One of the real advantages of this method of instruction is
that you can teach yourself to swim. *It is, in fact, my belief that
you, the fearful learner, should teach yourself to swim—with
proper guidance.* You are the one person who can deal most ef-

fectively with your fear, because only you know the exact limits of your fear, and it is you alone who can be patient enough to endure what may be a very long process of learning.

The beauty of teaching yourself is that there is no formal training, no strict regimentation. No one will rush you, no one will force you to do things you don't want to do, and no one will make impossible demands of you. And there is nobody to compete with. On the contrary, you will be entirely on your own! You will practice by yourself and at your own pace. You alone will decide what you can do and what you can't do.

So relax. This individualized instruction is designed just for you. Its unconventional approach eliminates much of the tension usually associated with formal swimming instruction. And it provides you, the fearful learner, with the most sympathetic teacher possible—yourself!

Keep It Casual

In the following chapters are my suggestions on how best to familiarize yourself with water and how to begin the process of learning to swim. They are the guidelines for your own individual learning program. They show you where and how to practice; you yourself can decide on the appropriateness of each suggestion. As you read the suggestions and eventually proceed through the lessons themselves, remember these few important hints:

First of all, try not to let the length of the book discourage you. The length is intended to clarify your relationship to water rather than to intimidate you. Don't frighten yourself by jumping ahead to later exercises (if you can't resist a quick glance, stay calm). The task that lies before you is not as impossible as it looks. Remember, it is only by proceeding slowly and step by step that this learning method works. So don't rush yourself. You are free to take as much time as you like with each lesson. Proceed at a pace that is comfortable for you. That is the whole idea behind this program.

Keep in mind that this is a very informal learning program. Do not go beyond your limits, but on the other hand don't be afraid to experiment either. If you encounter a particular lesson that gives you problems, forget it for a while and move on to a different lesson. You will become an excellent swimmer if you perform all the lessons in the order prescribed. It if should happen that you feel unable to perform *all* the lessons, instead of discarding the whole program, *be imaginative.* Design your own learning program. Skip around. Do the lessons you can, and leave the rest for later.

Give yourself a fair chance to learn to swim. Constantly remind yourself that there is nothing abnormal about being afraid of water. You have very good reason to be afraid. Fear is a natural human reaction to traumatic experience. You also have good reason for having retained your fear so long. Until now there has been no learning method appropriate to your needs—the world of swimmers has not bent over backwards to help you. And it is important to remember that you became a fearful nonswimmer through no fault of your own. So don't get down on yourself. You have been in a very difficult situation. You have been stuck with a problem that you were not responsible for and which until now had no apparent solution. If anything, you should be proud that in spite of your predicament you still have the desire to swim.

Don't let embarrassment prevent you from trying to learn on your own. You can always find some privacy, even on a crowded public beach. Besides, people don't notice you half as much as you think they do. Still, at the beginning you may be somewhat self-conscious about going to a public place to practice. That is only natural. But as you progress and gain more confidence, you will take less notice of other people and more notice of your own achievements. Just remember that you are on an important mission: You are teaching yourself to swim!

Finally, fear of water is a serious thing. I would never try to suggest that it isn't. But it is not as serious as you think. In fact, it can be pretty funny at times. So if I occasionally treat your fear lightly, remember that it is only because I want to help you. I want you to see your fear from a different perspective. I want you to think positively about yourself. I want you to know that *you can swim even though you are afraid of water.* That is why I emphasize your specific fears so much. Because only by breaking down your general fear of water into smaller, more manageable fears can we lighten your burden. And only by lightening your burden of fear and taking away some of its seriousness will you ever be able to defeat your fear of water. What I really want you to do, you see, is to surprise your fear and disarm it. I want you to say, "Okay. So I'm afraid of water. So what? Let's find a way to get me swimming anyhow!"

3
Getting Set
to Begin

Begin your learning program by finding a secure place to practice. Don't frighten yourself right from the very start. Look for a pleasant, very shallow body of water that you would feel comfortable in. And keep looking until you find one.

Your best bets are either an outdoor swimming pool or a lakeside beach. The shallow end of an outdoor pool is ideal, if it is *less* than 18 inches deep in the shallowest section. A public beach is also good if it offers a wide area of very shallow water. But be careful when considering a location. Confine your choice to lakes and outdoor pools. Stay away from indoor pools. They are usually dark and unpleasant. And never practice along river beaches. Rivers are too dangerous. And do not use an ocean beach unless (like a lagoon or inlet) it is completely sheltered from the surf.

When you find a shallow beach or pool to your liking, make absolutely sure that it is safe for you to be there. *Be certain that there are lifeguards or experienced, attentive swimmers in the area.* And make sure that the water conditions are good. The surface should be calm, with no currents and little or no wave action. The bottom should be nonrocky and smooth, so you can sit on it without discomfort. And the slope of the bottom should be gradual and even, with no holes or sudden drop-offs. The water itself should be relatively clean. Murky beach water is something you will just have to live with, but avoid places that are excessively muddy or filled with algae. Most important, make sure that there is a large area of very shallow water. Some swimming pools fail on this point because they are too deep even in the shallow end. The body of water you choose should have a large area that is less than 18 inches deep. That is very important.

This safe, secure, and very shallow area of water should also offer you some privacy. But it need not be a private location. Public places are fine. All that is necessary is that you be allowed to practice without interference.

When I was teaching myself to swim, I practiced at both a public beach and a public pool. The congestion did not interfere with my practice. At the lake it was easy to find privacy because very few people spent their time swimming in less than 2 feet of water. In fact, I was usually all alone, which was okay by me. The pool was much more crowded, because there was less area for everybody. But I don't remember having any problems. The people there were most often sympathetic and left me to myself. Public pools can, however, be more rowdy than public beaches. So check them out before you make your selection. Do not choose a public pool frequented by troublemakers. You don't need any harassment or criticism at the very beginning.

Finally, don't cheat when you make your selection. When I say "choose a shallow body of water you would feel comfortable in," I don't mean your bathtub. Do not practice in your bathtub or in the plastic kiddie pool you drag into the backyard every summer. You do have to find a safe, secure, and even cheerful body of water to practice in. But don't be ridiculous. Bathtubs and plastic pools are not appropriate. You are not afraid of your bathtub or your plastic kiddie pool. You are afraid of large bodies of water. And that means lakes and real swimming pools. So it is in that element that you should practice if you want to learn to swim despite your fear of water. Remember that *your goal is not to avoid large bodies of water, but to avoid fear in large bodies of water.*

What Aids to Use

You should know first of all that I *do not recommend* the use of flotation aids or locomotive aids. Wearing a life jacket or similar supporting device and skin-diving fins or hand paddles may at first seem a good idea, but I can assure you that using such artificial aids is really not wise. These aids can hinder your progress rather than help you. They promote dependency and give you a false sense of security. And they can aggravate your specific fears by allowing you to go into depths where you know you shouldn't be. In short, equipment of this sort does not tell you anything true about water or your own abilities in water.

But there are a few artificial aids that I do recommend. These are *noseplugs, goggles,* and *skin-diving masks.* Unlike flotation aids and locomotive aids, these items do not aggravate your specific fears or give you a false sense of security. All they do is provide a useful function: they permit you to avoid those few specific fears that cannot be avoided by any other means. Fear of loss of eyesight or fear of getting water in your eyes or up your nose are fears you might experience if you didn't wear goggles, noseplugs, or a mask. There is no way that common sense alone could help you avoid those fears, because it is inevitable that as you learn to swim water will splash in your face or your face will become submerged. But by using these artificial aids you will *not experience* those specific fears. Water will not be permitted to get in your eyes or up your nose. These three aids, then, promote the possibility of your success rather than hinder it. They provide you with a way to work around three of your specific fears, which would otherwise be obstacles in your effort to become a swimmer.

So take this advice. If you are afraid of getting water up your nose, try wearing noseplugs. If you are afraid of the loss of eyesight when your head is submerged and afraid to open your eyes, wear goggles. If you have both nose- and eye-related fears, wear both noseplugs and goggles. Or try wearing a skin-diving mask. The mask is probably the better choice because it avoids all your nose- and eye-related fears with one single piece of equipment. But if you think you would look too silly wearing a skin-diving mask, stick with the noseplugs and goggles. In either case you will leave only your mouth exposed to water, so you will have only one specific fear to worry about—fear of choking, which you can deal with initially by keeping your mouth closed when your face is in or almost in the water. And that reduction of potential fears should make your experience with water much easier to endure. Whichever you choose, however, be sure that it is good quality equipment. Very inexpensive goggles and masks often do not fit properly or function well. They sometimes leak and are often uncomfortable. So get the best equipment that you can afford. You won't be sorry.

4

Water Familiarity

By now you have selected a beach or pool around which you feel secure. It has a wide area of shallow water about 18 inches deep or less. There are no currents and very little if any wave action. Great.

Now let's start to get you familiar with the water. We won't need the mask, goggles, or noseplugs for a while. So leave them on the shore or the edge of the pool. We're just going to play around for now.

STEP 1

Wade into the water, about up to your ankles. If you are in a pool and the shallowest part is 18 inches deep, that's fine. Eighteen inches deep is only about knee deep. Now sit in the water. That's right, *sit in it.* Don't cheat. It's not too cold, is it? And it is certainly not too deep. Just sit there for a while—as long as you want to, actually. Try to relax a bit. Splash around, if you like. Enjoy yourself. There is certainly nothing to be afraid of at this depth.

Okay, if you feel somewhat comfortable sitting in ankle-deep water, move on to knee-deep water, gradually if necessary, and sit in it. If you are already in knee-deep water, stay there. Again, relax as much as you can. It's not deep at all. Nothing horrid can happen to you here. You're perfectly safe. Play with the water, splash it, try to loosen up. Consider the water itself. At this shallow depth it is certainly not your enemy.

Are you relaxed? If you aren't yet, just keep playing around until you are relaxed. If you are relaxed, we're going to proceed with getting you accustomed to the water. *But we will not go any deeper.* That's something I'm sure you appreciate. Where you sit now is where we are going to practice for a long time. There is no need to go any farther into the water. *You can learn to swim in knee-deep water!*

STEP 2

You may have noticed while sitting in this knee-deep water that you can easily touch bottom with your hands. Feel it. Pretty nice to know it's there, huh? I want you to get accustomed to putting your hands on the bottom. It is a very important part of my teaching method.

Place your hands beside you, with your arms fully extended and your palms flat on the bottom. If the water touches your armpits, you are too deep. Move back into shallower water. The water surface should lie about 2 inches below your armpits. Look around. Familiarize yourself with this location. From now on when I refer to knee-deep or arm-length water, I am referring to this depth (see figure 1).

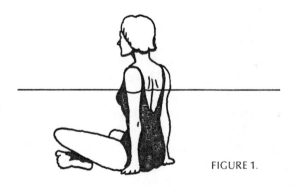

FIGURE 1.

Now place your hands behind you and lean backward a little bit. Don't put your head in the water, just sort of lean back. Then place your hands in front of you, and lean forward. Do that often. Practice placing your hands behind and in front of you, leaning slightly backwards and forwards (see figures 2 and 3). You will probably feel more comfortable leaning forward than backward, so practice that more, and let the water come up higher. Let the water splash your shoulders. When you aren't afraid to let the water touch your neck, you are ready for the next step.

FIGURE 2.

FIGURE 3.

STEP 3

You should still be sitting in knee-deep water, relaxing and practicing leaning backward and forward with your hands on the bottom. Now "walk around" on your hands. Lean forward, placing your hands in front of you, letting the water touch your shoulders, just as you have been doing (see figure 3). Good. Now rise up off your posterior, get on your knees (see figure 4), and

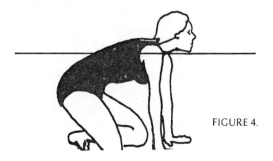

FIGURE 4.

let your legs slide through to the back of you. Let your legs stretch out and touch the bottom. You should now be in the prone position (see figure 5) with your hands about 12 inches apart on the bottom, with only your head, neck, shoulders, and tops of your arms out of the water. Now start walking around on your hands, staying at this same depth, which should be almost arm length when you are in the prone position. Face forward, keeping your head entirely clear of the water, and breathe normally. You can "walk" into shallower water if that makes you feel more comfortable, but try to relax in this arm-length water. You should look like the person in figure 6.

Prone position

FIGURE 5.

"Walking"

FIGURE 6.

STEP 4

Familiarize yourself with this prone position. Relax as much as you can. The water is shallow enough so that you should not have to strain to keep your head above water. And it is not necessary to keep your arms straight. You can bend your elbows. Your chin will still be clear of the water. So loosen up. This is the position you will use continuously. From this position you will learn to swim.

Walk around on your hands until you are completely relaxed in this movement. If you pull yourself around fast enough, you will notice that your legs rise up off the bottom and that you are actually pulling your whole body around in the water! When you get this far, you've got it made. You are relaxed enough to let your legs float a little. Very good. (See figure 7.)

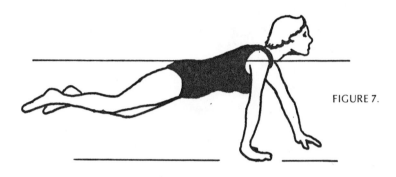

FIGURE 7.

STEP 5

Hey, hey! Guess what you can do now! While you pull yourself around in this shallow water, dragging your legs behind you, you can *start kicking your legs*. Leave your hands on the bottom, of course, so your head stays completely out of the water, but start kicking your legs instead of letting them lie there motionless. Kick with your whole leg, not just from the knee down. Move your legs up and down in the water in a "scissors" action. When one leg kicks down in the water, the other should be going up to get ready to kick down again. Pretend that you're really swimming! You will find that your legs tend to rise toward the surface when you kick them like that. That's the whole idea behind the leg kick. But don't let that frighten you. You're not going anyplace—your hands are still on the bottom.

Practice this for a long time. Get relaxed at doing the leg kick while you walk around on your hands. You should be looking

FIGURE 8.

like figure 8. When you can do all this without fear, you have achieved "water familiarization" and are ready to learn "buoyancy." Congratulations!

5
Getting You Buoyant in Arm-length Water

In case you hadn't noticed, you have almost achieved buoyancy already. By "walking" on your hands and kicking with your legs, you have permitted your waist and legs to rise to the surface. Now all we have to do is get your front half buoyant!

STEP 1

Get your mask or goggles and noseplugs now and return to your favorite spot in knee-deep water. Don't get back into the prone position yet. For now just sit in the water.

We are *not* going to put your head under water, so don't worry about that. Such feats come much later. I simply want you to wear these artificial aids at this time as a precaution against fear. In the process of learning buoyancy you may splash some water in your face. So, if that would frighten you, wear the mask or goggles and noseplugs now. We want to work around those specific fears, especially at this early stage of learning.

The goggles or mask should be fitted tightly enough so that water can't get in, but they shouldn't be so tight that they hurt your head. The same applies to the noseplugs. They should be snug, but not painful. When you get these aids properly fitted (see figures 9 and 10), try splashing some water in your face. If there are no leaks, the equipment is fitted well. By the way, it

A good mask will have a tempered glass window, metal rims, a stiff rubber body, a soft rubber cushion that fits the contour of your face, and buckles for strap adjustment. The mask completely covers the eyes and nose, which means it fits against the forehead, temples, sides of cheeks, and under the nose.

FIGURE 9.

A good pair of goggles should fit snugly around the eye cavities. Goggles with plenty of rubber between the windows and your eyes provide the best protection. Avoid very inexpensive goggles. Double straps are recommended for both mask and goggles.

FIGURE 10.

wasn't so bad getting a little water on the face, was it? Maybe even fun? You can see just fine, and no water gets in your eyes or up your nose. Very good.

STEP 2

You should now be sitting in knee-deep water with your mask or goggles and noseplugs in place. We now begin the process of getting your front half buoyant. What we eventually want to do by the end of this chapter is to achieve buoyancy without the support of your hands on the bottom. That may at first sound terribly frightening, but just remember that you are in very shallow water. It is only arm-length deep, so don't worry. You can at any time support yourself by simply reaching for the bottom with your hands. Achieving buoyancy can, however, be a difficult and long process. So you must be patient with yourself.

While you are sitting there in the water, let's experiment with hand shapes. Many people think that a cupped hand pushes the water around more effectively than an opened hand. But that is not true. The opened hand is much more effective. You can prove it yourself. Bring your fingers together in a cup shape with your thumb placed against your forefinger. Having formed cups with both hands, run those cups through the water. Then try it without cupping your hands. Open your hands, separating your fingers *slightly,* and push the water back and forth. Feel how opened hands push the water around much more forcefully than cupped hands. That is an important lesson. The easiest hand shape for learning every swimming stroke is the fingers-open shape (see figure 11).*

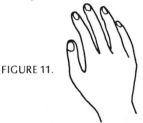

FIGURE 11.

Now, instead of pushing the water around any which way, place your hands at your sides, and alternating with each arm, push the water straight down from the surface to the bottom with your open hands. As you raise one hand to the surface, the other should be forcing its way to the bottom. You should be looking something like a two-cylinder engine with two pistons alternately going up and down (see figure 12). Practice this for a while. You are doing fine.

FIGURE 12.

*Some instructors and instruction manuals recommend the open hand shape with the fingers held together. It is my experience that a hand with fingers spread *slightly* actually provides a wider paddling surface than a hand with fingers together. Also, the effort made consciously by a novice to hold the fingers together often creates unnecessary tension in the arms at a time when any strained movement is particularly counterproductive.

STEP 3

Okay. Get back into the prone position with your hands on the bottom. You don't have to kick your legs for this exercise. Just let them lie still for now. While your hands are on the bottom, they should be in a relaxed position. They should be about 10 or 12 inches apart, and each hand should be lying flat with the fingers slightly separated and the thumb spread for support (see figure 13). When you feel comfortable, raise one hand to

FIGURE 13.

the surface in front of you and look at it. Your raised hand should still be in the palm-down position, but it should be on top of the water, about 8 inches from your face (see figure 14). Your entire body should be balancing on one arm and two legs, so you should have no problem keeping your head completely out of water. At that point, force your hand back down to the bottom, pushing the water down just as you did when you were in the sitting position. Now do the same with the other hand, raising it to the surface and then pushing the water down from the surface to the bottom. Now, always leaving one hand on the bottom, begin the "piston action" of your arms again. Bring one hand at a time up to the surface and then force it back down to the bottom (see figures 15 and 16). When the left hand touches bottom, raise the right hand to the surface and push the water back to the bottom. When the right hand touches bottom, raise the left hand to the surface, and so on. You should be feeling the pushing action, just as you did when you were sitting down. Feel

FIGURE 14.

FIGURE 15.

Piston action in the prone position

FIGURE 16.

how you seem to push the water down with your hands. You are doing very well. Keep practicing this piston action in the prone position. When you feel quite comfortable with this exercise, move on to step 4.

STEP 4

Remain in the prone position with your hands on the bottom. Your legs still should be stretched out behind you, lying motionless on the bottom. Your head should be completely out of the water and you should be breathing normally. If you are wearing a skin-diving mask or noseplugs, you are, of course, breathing through your mouth. But if you are not using either of those two aids, begin breathing through your mouth anyway. *Do not breathe with your nose.* For now, forget you even have a nose. And if water should happen to splash into your mouth, don't inhale. Just spit it out and then continue breathing normally.

Start now doing the piston action again with your arms. Alternating with each hand, push the water back down to the bottom. Let your hands rise to a point near the surface, but no longer let them come completely out of the water. The piston action of your arms and hands should now take place entirely beneath the surface (see figure 17). Pick up the tempo a bit. Increase the speed of your piston action. When one hand touches bottom, quickly raise the other hand toward the surface, and then push more water back to the bottom. Get as coordinated as you possibly can at this. Pretend it's a relay race. When one hand touches the bottom, the other hand should quickly reach toward the surface water.

Start now to kick your legs, just as you did when you were walking around on your hands. Kick with the whole leg, not just from the knees down. Your waist and legs should be becoming buoyant, and you still should be doing a quick-piston action with your hands (see figure 18). If this poses problems of coordination for you, *keep practicing until you feel comfortable at moving both your legs and arms at the same time.* Even when you feel comfortable at this exercise, keep practicing it. The legs should be kicking, keeping your waist and legs buoyant; and your arms should be doing a quick-piston action, one hand reaching near the surface water just as the other touches bottom. This is an extremely important exercise. You are not buoyant yet, but you soon will be.

STEP 5

Okay. By now you should be accustomed to breathing through your mouth and somewhat accustomed to the feel of the mask or goggles and noseplugs. The advantage you gain by

FIGURE 17.

The hands no longer rise above the waterline during the piston action.

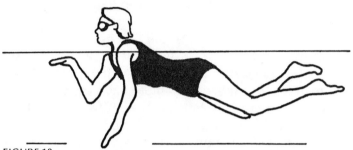

FIGURE 18.

Combining the piston action with the leg kick

wearing these aids is obvious: You don't have to worry about your eyes or nose, you only have to worry about getting water in your mouth. And I know you've been careful about that. We are now going to try to get you completely buoyant, however; and because that involves the coordination of "front buoyancy" and "rear buoyancy," it can be very difficult. So I suggest that during these brief attempts at "total buoyancy"—and they will be only brief—you close your mouth and hold your breath.

Now don't panic. There is nothing to be afraid of. You aren't going to sink! You are already familiar with the piston action of your hands, and you have already achieved waist and leg buoyancy by kicking your legs. All we are going to do now is to combine those two exercises and to try to get you completely buoyant. And remember that you are in very shallow water. *You can't sink!* All you have to do to recover from a brief attempt at total buoyancy is put your hands on the bottom! So don't panic. The whole procedure is perfectly safe.

Let's try it. Get back into the water in the prone position with your hands on the bottom, and breathe normally through your mouth. Get the arms and hands going again in the piston action. Start kicking your legs in the manner prescribed. As you feel your waist and legs become buoyant, increase the speed of the piston action. When one hand touches bottom, immediately raise the other hand toward the surface and push the water back down to the bottom. Keep this up. Do it faster and faster! Anticipate when one hand will touch bottom and raise the other toward the surface just before the first one touches bottom. Keep this good piston action going. And keep the legs kicking, too. Now close your mouth and hold your breath. Ready for lift-off! This is it! *Increase the speed of the leg kicks and the arm piston action.* Faster, faster! Rely less and less on the bottom for support and more and more on your piston action for support. When you feel the piston action beginning to support you in the water, increase your speed even more and forget about the bottom entirely. Don't touch bottom at all (see figure 19)! As each hand nears the bottom, quickly raise it back up toward the surface! *Let your piston action support your front half entirely!* Do the piston action in the water between the surface and the bottom, but don't touch either! Keep going. Faster, faster! You're buoyant!!!

FIGURE 19.
Buoyancy

Did you make it? If you did, good! But keep practicing it again and again. If you didn't make it, don't worry. Hardly anyone achieves buoyancy on their first try. It took me considerable practice before I did it. It is not necessary for your very first attempt at total buoyancy to be entirely successful. All I ask is that you get the idea of how it works—how total buoyancy *can* be achieved. And I want you to get comfortable with the process of catching yourself by simply reaching for the bottom with your hands. A certain amount of experimentation on your own part is necessary, too. You have to learn just how much force it takes to hold each half up.

Coordination can be a problem. It's not easy to keep both halves of your body buoyant at the same time. If you slack off on either your front or rear half, or just forget about one of the halves, that half is going to sink. That is why it is especially important in these early learning stages to practice in shallow water. If your back half doesn't maintain buoyancy, all that happens is that your legs come to rest on the bottom. If your front half doesn't stay buoyant—if, for example, you can't seem to push the water down fast enough—all you have to do is catch yourself by putting your hands on the bottom. It may be difficult to achieve total buoyancy, but because you are learning in a completely safe environment, you can afford to try over and over again.

The next time you attempt total buoyancy—and you should keep trying until you succeed—follow these suggestions: When you release your contact with the bottom as you increase the speed of the piston action, the downward strokes of your arms and hands should become shorter. The faster the piston action is, the shorter the strokes should become, until ultimately your front half is being kept buoyant by very fast, very short strokes.

Practice over and over again. Remember, you are your own teacher. Decide what you need to work on, and then practice until you get it right. If you have had problems at any time up to this point, just go back over the information already offered.

Achieving total buoyancy is rewarding, but it's also difficult. You may have failed this time, and you may continue to fail after many attempts. *But at some point you will succeed.* Your success with buoyancy will at first come in brief spurts. You will become buoyant for a few seconds, then catch yourself with your hands on the bottom, and then experience another brief moment of buoyancy. But as you continue to practice, the experiences of buoyancy will become longer and more frequent. You will become able to maintain buoyancy for longer intervals. When you finally can maintain buoyancy for a continuous period of time—and are terribly proud of yourself and even dare to breathe normally while maintaining buoyancy—that is when you will be ready for the next chapter.

6
Now Swim

You have now achieved total buoyancy, and you should be very proud of yourself. Maintaining buoyancy should assure you that you can, with effort, defeat this demon water. *Even you can learn to stay atop the water.* And though you may still be afraid, you have gained enough confidence to start thinking about the possibility of swimming.

Now that you have gained confidence in your ability to maintain buoyancy under secure conditions, you should try to gain that same confidence in your ability to swim under secure conditions. It is only by confidence in your own abilities that you will ever rid yourself of your fear of water. So keep up the good work.

STEP 1

The transition from buoyancy to swimming is not difficult. In case you hadn't noticed, you are practically swimming already. You have learned to maintain buoyancy, and now need only learn to move through the water while maintaining buoyancy.

So get back into knee-deep water. Don't forget to wear the mask or goggles and noseplug if you think you need them. Become totally buoyant again. The kicking of your legs and the piston action of your arms and hands should be keeping both your front and rear halves buoyant. Breathe as normally as possible while maintaining total buoyancy.

Even though you are now totally buoyant, you are not moving. To move through the water instead of remaining in place, make one simple change. *Change the pattern of the piston action of your arms and hands.* Instead of making a strictly vertical motion with your hands, start making a circular motion. Pretend you are peddling a bicycle with your arms under water. Your hands should still be alternating their movement; when one is reaching up, the other should be pushing down. But instead of simply moving up and down, *your hands should now make a circular motion. They should reach up and forward* and then pull *down and back.* The trick is to reach forward and pull the water down and toward you (see figure 20).   kick legs

You should now be moving. Don't let it frighten you. Your head is still above the water, and you can breathe normally. Remember to stay in very shallow water. Do not point yourself toward deeper water. To catch yourself you need only reach bottom with your hands. If you are making the proper arm and leg movements, you should look like figure 21.

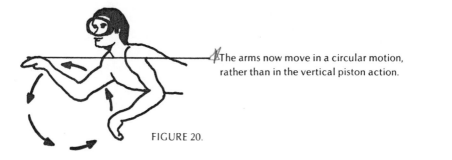

The arms now move in a circular motion, rather than in the vertical piston action.

FIGURE 20.

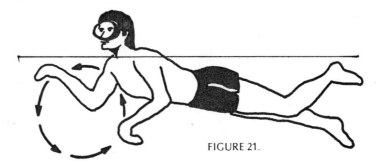

FIGURE 21.

STEP 2

Congratulations. You have just learned the elementary dog paddle and are now swimming! And you thought it could never be done. You probably are not confident yet of your new ability, so keep practicing.

The elementary dog paddle is probably the most instinctive stroke in swimming. But even the dog paddle requires practice. If you have ever seen a dog swim, you know how the stroke functions. It is a continuous and circular movement beneath the surface of the water. The swimmer reaches up and forward with the hands, then pushes the water down and pulls it toward him. When you practice, don't forget to keep the palms of your hands down. And remember to kick your legs.

Practice the dog paddle again and again. Get so comfortable with it that you can paddle about the shallows with confidence. The fun of swimming in a secure environment soon will enable you to progress even beyond the dog paddle. When you dog-paddle with confidence, move on to the next chapter.

7
From the Dog Paddle to the Crawl in Shallow Water

The purpose of the previous lessons was to get you into the water and swimming. At the same time, I wanted you to feel more self-assured in water. Of course, without a certain amount of confidence you would not have gotten this far, and each time you progress to the next lesson, your confidence in your own ability probably increases by leaps and bounds. So with each chapter you are probably becoming more relaxed in the water. But if you are not, make a conscious effort to loosen up. It is very important that you try to relax as much as possible.

The lessons that follow can be difficult to learn, if only because the information offered is heavily detailed. So take your time. *Study each lesson thoroughly on dry land before entering the water to practice.* If you are patient with yourself and do not attempt to rush through each lesson, your practice should be both rewarding and enjoyable.

STEP 1

You have learned the elementary dog paddle. Keep practicing that stroke until you are proficient at it. It is very good exercise, and it also helps you relax and become more confident in the water. If you are performing the dog paddle correctly, you should look like figure 22. Your head should be completely out of the water, and you should be breathing normally through your mouth. Your arms should move in a continuous circular motion beneath the surface of the water, with your hands — palms down — reaching up and forward and forcing the water down and towards you. As you become better at the dog paddle, the circular strokes should become smaller and less frantic. And don't forget to kick your legs. Try to enjoy the sensation of moving through the water.

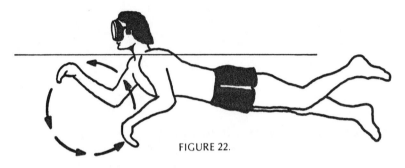

FIGURE 22.

The elementary dog paddle

STEP 2

By this lesson you should be pretty good at the elementary dog paddle. We are now going to learn a second type of dog paddle. Let's call it the egg-shape dog paddle. There will be very little change in movement except for a slight exaggeration in the arm stroke. Instead of performing rather small circular movements with your arms and hands, try now to make an elliptical or oval motion (see figure 23). *Reach farther out in front of you and pull the water right back towards your chest.* Instead of pushing the water down with your hands and then pulling it towards you in a very even circular motion, *put less emphasis on pushing the water down* and *put more emphasis on pulling the water towards you.*

This transition should not be a difficult one for you to make. You can already perform the elementary dog paddle. And the

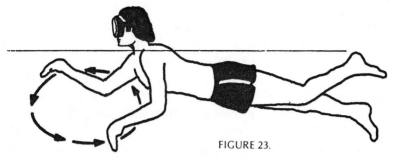

FIGURE 23.

The egg-shape dog paddle. The circular motion changes to a spherical motion. But everything else stays the same. The head is still above the water, so you should be breathing normally through your mouth.

egg-shape dog paddle is virtually the same thing. The entire arm stroke remains beneath the surface of the water. I only ask you now to extend your reach in front of you, and when you pull the water with your hands back towards you, follow a shallower path—don't go as deep with your pulling strokes. Your reaching strokes should be almost a straight line from your chest, and your pulling strokes should not be as deep as they were while performing the elementary dog paddle.

Practice this stroke until you feel comfortable with it. You will notice that this exaggeration in arm movement allows you to move faster through the water. If this pleases you, good. If it frightens you, keep practicing until you feel comfortable with this new stroke. Remember to stay in very shallow water where you need only touch bottom with your hands to catch yourself.

STEP 3

In learning the egg-shape dog paddle, your reaching stroke became longer and more horizontal, and your pulling stroke also became more horizontal, with more emphasis on pulling the water back towards you than pushing the water down. The whole stroke, if viewed from the side, became more elliptical than circular.

We are now going to learn a third type of dog paddle. Let's call this one the triangular dog paddle, because the arm strokes become even more exaggerated and resemble the shape of a triangle, but the entire stroke is still performed beneath the water line. The reaching stroke remains the same, except that you should *extend your arms until they are completely straight.* When you reach for the water in front of you it should be a horizontal motion, with your arms extended as far as possible. The pulling stroke, however, undergoes a radical change: instead of pulling the water back towards your chest, *pull the water back towards the sides of your body.* And instead of making the pulling stroke horizontal to the water surface, make it come down at an angle. With your arms stretched out before you, grab the surface water with your hands and pull it straight back to about 18 inches beneath the side of your body. It should be a straight line from the surface water to below your rib cage (see figures 24 and 25).

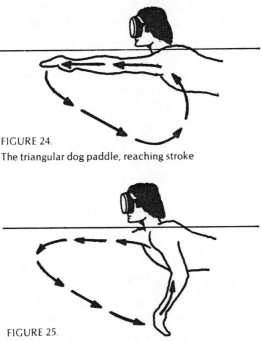

FIGURE 24.
The triangular dog paddle, reaching stroke

FIGURE 25.
The triangular dog paddle, pulling stroke

From the side view, the arm stroke should resemble the shape of a bicycle chain. The reaching stroke should still be a horizontal motion, but the arm should become fully extended just before you begin each pulling stroke. When the elbow bends, the hand should pull the water back to a point about 18 inches below your rib cage—or about half the length of your body. At this point your arm should be roughly vertical to the surface water and your hand should be pushing the water behind you. The idea is first to pull the water towards your sides and then push it past you. After pushing the water behind you, raise your hand toward the surface and immediately perform another horizontal reaching stroke. This cycle is, of course, repeated over and over.

This is a very crucial stroke in the transition from the elementary dog paddle to the crawl, so be certain you understand how it works. The major difference is the pulling stroke: Instead of pulling the water back to your chest, you pull the water back to beneath your ribs. This causes changes: The pulling stroke becomes deeper the farther you pull back, and it also becomes a wider stroke because you are bringing your hands to a point beneath the sides of your body instead of the front. Figures 26 and 27, showing both a top and side view, illustrate what I mean.

FIGURE 26.

The triangular dog paddle. From the side, this stroke appears more triangular than spherical, but the head position and leg kick remain the same.

FIGURE 27.

The triangular dog paddle. Viewed from above, the stroke widens as you pull the water down and back below your rib cage.

STEP 4

The last lesson provided us with a stroke that was—as viewed from the side—more triangular than egg-shaped. And viewed from the top, the strokes no longer ran parallel, but widened as they pulled the water back. If you think you are not performing this stroke correctly, go back to step 3 and practice more. It is important that you do it right. We are now deep into your learning program, and it is best to take your time and perform each step properly.

This triangular dog paddle should now be refined a bit. And in doing so, we create another stroke. Let's call it the *full-stroke dog paddle.* If you are comfortable with the triangular dog paddle, make the following changes: When you perform the reaching stroke, make an effort to extend your arms farther than you have been doing. Move your shoulders as you alternate reaching with your left and right arms. When you reach with your right arm, drop your left shoulder back a bit and bring your right shoulder forward, allowing you to reach even farther with your right arm. When you reach forward with your left arm, bring your left shoulder forward and drop your right shoulder back. Your shoulders should now become participants in the swimming strokes (see figure 28). But your arms and hands should still remain below the waterline.

The pulling stroke should be lengthened also. Rather than stopping your arms beneath the midpoint of your body, follow through so that your arms again become parallel to the rest of your body. Pull the water back to a point beneath your ribs, and then continue to push the water back until your hands reach the area of your hips. *Instead of making a half stroke, follow through and make a full stroke with your arms.* Push the water to a point behind your hips (see figure 29).

You will find that even though the arm strokes now take more time to complete, you are propelling yourself through the water at a faster pace. The strokes are now full-length strokes, and they naturally take more effort and more time to perform. But because they are longer, they are more efficient strokes. They propel you through the water faster than the variety of shorter

FIGURE 28.
The full-stroke dog paddle, reaching stroke

FIGURE 29.
The full-stroke dog paddle, pulling stroke

strokes we have learned. And because they are more efficient strokes, it takes fewer of them to keep you moving through the water. So relax as much as possible and continue to practice. This is a very important stroke for you to master.

STEP 5

In step 6 we will have you doing the crawl stroke. You are almost performing it now. But before we do that, let's go back and do some work on your leg kick. We have been neglecting your rear half.

If you have succeeded in getting this far, you have been doing something right. You have learned to maintain total buoyancy and even to propel yourself through the water using several varieties of the dog paddle. So (unless you have been cheating) your leg kick has been satisfactory. Now, however, we are in transition from the dog paddle to the crawl stroke. Since we are in the process of tuning up your arm strokes, let's see if we can improve your leg kick as well.

Get back into the prone position in shallow water. With your hands on the bottom supporting your entire body, practice your leg kick. The idea of the leg kick is to *push the water down,* thus forcing your rear half to rise in the water. Use your whole leg when you kick, not just from your knees down. You can bend your knees, of course, but think in terms of your whole leg when you kick. Even your ankles should participate in the leg kick. Let your ankles relax when you kick, thus allowing your feet to function as paddles at the end of your legs. You will at first be inclined to kick too fast and too hard, but try to relax and slow your kick down, keeping in mind the elements of a proper leg kick. *If you use your whole leg when you kick, and maintain flexibility at the knees and ankles, your leg kick will become much more efficient and much less of an effort.* You will find that an efficient leg kick will keep your waist and legs buoyant better and with less work. And a good leg kick has an added benefit: it propels you through the water faster. And the faster you move through the water, the less effort it takes to keep you buoyant. All of which means, the more efficient your leg kick, the less work it will be for you to become a better swimmer.

STEP 6

Okay, up to now all of your arm strokes should have been performed under the water. At no time during the elementary dog paddle, the egg-shape dog paddle, the triangular dog paddle, or the full-stroke dog paddle should your arms or hands have come out of the water, although the reaching strokes should have come very near the surface. The efficiency of your arm stroke improved each time you progressed to the next stroke, but the strokes themselves have been performed at or beneath the surface of the water.

You are now ready to learn the crawl stroke. With the crawl stroke, for the first time, you will break the surface of the water with your arms and hands. The crawl is basically the same as the full-stroke dog paddle with the exception that *the arms and hands come out of the water on the reaching strokes.* The transition to the crawl should not be difficult if you have learned to perform the full-stroke dog paddle as described in step 4.

FIGURE 30.

FIGURE 31.

FIGURE 32.

FIGURE 33.

The crawl stroke. The crawl is almost identical to the full-stroke dog paddle. Only the reaching stroke changes as the arm reaches forward *out of the water.*

The leg kick remains the same. The pulling strokes also remain the same—they should be full-length strokes. The reaching stroke is all that changes. Instead of reaching horizontally just beneath the surface of the water, bring your arms and hands out of the water. Here's how it works:

At the completion of the full-length pulling stroke, bend your elbow and bring first your arm and then your hand out of the water as you reach forward (see figure 30). At midpoint during the reaching stroke, your arm and hand should both be completely out of the water (see figure 31). As you bring your arm forward, let first your hand and then your arm re-enter the water at a point approximately 2 feet in front of your shoulder (see figure 32). Then, with arm and hand reaching into the surface water, straighten your arm, extend it as usual to its full length, and begin another pulling stroke (see figure 33). The whole stroke should be performed as smoothly and rhythmically as possible. The series of illustrations shown should be very useful to you. Practice repeatedly after you understand the procedure.

STEP 7

About this time you may be wondering what you are supposed to do with your head when you are learning the crawl stroke. You may be worrying about whether I'm going to make you submerge your head in the water and then teach you rhythmic breathing. Well, don't worry. Most swimming instructors do teach the crawl that way, but you are not ready yet to submerge your head in water. So we will continue our policy of ignoring tradition and do the crawl our own way. Breathe as you have been doing with the other swimming strokes. Leave your head out of the water and breathe normally through your mouth. Let your arm strokes and leg kicks keep your head supported completely above water.

At first this may prove a bit awkward, and that is a good sign that you are performing the crawl arm strokes correctly. Your shoulders will turn as you alternately reach with your left and right arms. When you reach with your right arm, your right shoulder will go forward; and when you reach with your left arm, your left shoulder will go forward. This turning action of your shoulders will have an effect on your head and neck — they will want to turn also. If it feels natural to turn your head as you turn your shoulders, do so. But if it feels more comfortable to keep your head stationary, looking straight forward, do that. Do whichever feels more comfortable to you (see figure 34).

So when you practice the crawl stroke you have two choices: You can either look like Lloyd Bridges in "Sea Hunt" reruns and turn your head as you turn your shoulders, or else you can make

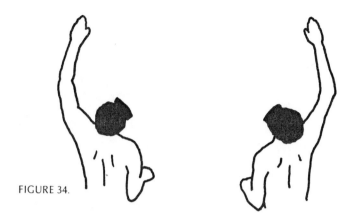

FIGURE 34.

You may want to turn your head as you shift your arms and shoulders.

like Johnny Weissmuller in old *Tarzan* movies and keep your head stationary while you do the crawl. The choice is yours to make. The important thing is to keep your head up and breathe normally. The time will come (much later) for you to learn the proper rhythmic breathing method for the crawl stroke, but by then you will be a very confident swimmer.

STEP 8

I have given you the rudiments of the crawl stroke. With this information you can become a good swimmer. How fast you proceed and how well you learn, however, are largely up to you. It may take a long time to become skilled at this stroke we call the crawl. On the other hand, it may not take you very long at all. The important thing is to practice diligently! When, after many, many practice sessions you come to feel confident with the crawl stroke in shallow water, you will have come a long way. If you work hard and practice continuously, your water skills will now grow by leaps and bounds.

8
Go Deeper

We now come to something that is probably going to scare you. We are going to have you practice swimming in deeper water. It will, however, be a very gradual process. First you'll swim in knee-deep water, then in waist-deep water, and finally in chest-deep water. As I say, this may well be frightening for you. But it is an essential lesson, something that you will have to encounter at some time if you are ever going to be a confident swimmer. So let's encounter it now. And take heart. *If you have successfully performed the previous lessons, you are ready for deeper water.*

Even though deeper water is a frightening subject, there are ways of lessening that fear. For one thing, remember your mission. You are trying to learn to swim, and that means — eventually — deeper water. Wouldn't you rather experience it now, while you are combating your fear of water anyway, rather than at some surprising or accidental time in the future? And besides, it's not as though you are going into this thing cold. You can already attain buoyancy and even swim in shallow water; you have learned to stay on top of the water. All I ask is that you practice what you have already learned, but now in deeper water instead of knee-deep water. You are equipped to swim in deeper water. All you need is courage.

There are physical adjustments you can make so that deeper water will be more bearable. For example, I will not ask you to just plunge into deeper water straight out. As I said before, it will be a gradual introduction. And I will show you ways to make that gradual introduction easier. Just as in previous lessons, we are going to work around as many of your specific fears as possible. We will try to eliminate most of the problems that lie between you and deeper water. But you will have to encounter one specific fear—deeper water. Even though you are ready for it physically, you have to deal with it emotionally on your own. *You can swim.* Now you must prove to yourself that you can battle this fear and swim in deeper water.

I never said that there would not be times when you had to be courageous. I provide the instructional method that enables you to work around your fears as much as possible. But when courage becomes necessary, only you can provide that.

STEP 1

If you are using a swimming pool, get into the shallow end and, *holding onto the side of the pool,* walk out to chest-deep water. If you are at the beach, look for a dock that has something secure to hold onto—a handrail for example, or a horizontal two-by-four support beam, or the edge of the dock itself. Holding onto the dock for support, walk out into chest-deep water. But make sure that whatever you are using for a handrail is secure. Do not use a rope, a loose piling support, a tree branch, or anything like that. The handrail should be something stationary and solid.

Stand there awhile in the chest-deep water. Try to relax a little, although that may be difficult. All we are going to do for now is practice your leg kick, so *don't panic.* The leg kick is something you can always use more practice on. Loosen up, if you can. You're not going to sink.

Face the edge of the pool or the dock, and with both hands grasp whatever you are using for a handrail. Then move back about an arm length from the handrail (see figure 35). Push off from the bottom with your feet and let your whole body stretch straight out in the water. Concentrate on becoming horizontal if

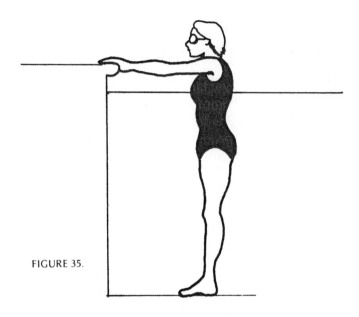

FIGURE 35.

your body isn't floating by itself into a horizontal position. Start kicking your legs. Use your whole leg when you kick, from your hips to your feet. Don't forget that the idea is to push the water down with your legs, so put more emphasis on the downward thrust of your leg kick (see figure 36).

You should be completely horizontal now, with your leg kicks causing your rear half to become buoyant, and the handrail supporting your front half. Relax as much as possible. Experiment with the leg kick. Feel it out. Test just what amount of effort you must make to keep your legs and waist buoyant. Kick slower and faster, make subtle changes in the shape of your legs—see how the leg kick works and which way it works best. You will discover that a good leg kick does not require splashing. There is no need to break the surface with your feet. The most effective kick is one that works entirely under water, with the legs raised to a point near—but not above—the surface just before the downward thrust.

Practice this lesson repeatedly. Get as comfortable as possible with it.

STEP 2

Walk back into knee-deep water now. This time, however, get into knee-deep water that is nearer your handrail. If you are at the beach, for example, get about 6 feet away from the dock. If you are in a pool, get about 6 feet away from the edge of the pool. Now get into your prone position with your hands on the bottom and face the handrail. Push yourself off from the bottom with your hands and do the crawl stroke as you normally would, but instead of catching yourself by placing your hands on the bottom, catch yourself by grasping the handrail (see figure 37). When you grasp the handrail, stop your leg kicks as

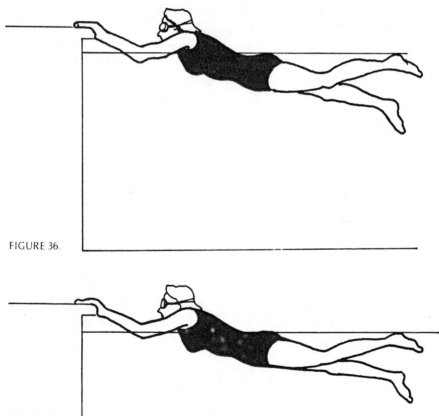

FIGURE 36.

FIGURE 37.
Grasping the handrail is your new method of recovery. Instead of placing your hands on the bottom, reach for the dock or poolside.

well as your arm strokes and let your legs touch bottom. Then stand up. Go back to your starting point about 6 feet from the handrail, get back into the prone position, and swim to the handrail again. Do not touch bottom with your hands during your brief swim to the handrail. Repeat this lesson over and over again in knee-deep water. Swim to the handrail and then walk back to your beginning position. You should be doing the crawl when you swim to the handrail. Don't fudge.

STEP 3

Move your starting point back to about 10 feet from the handrail. The entire 10 feet should still be in only knee-deep water. Follow the same procedure as in step 2. Get into the prone position with your hands on the bottom. Swim to the handrail, grasp it, and then stand up and walk back to your starting point. The only difference is that you are swimming a longer distance through the water. At no time during your 10-foot swim should you support yourself by touching bottom with your hands. Practice swimming this distance until you feel comfortable with it.

STEP 4

Move your starting point back farther. Make it about 15 feet from the handrail. Follow the same procedure: swim to the handrail, grasp it, and then walk back to your starting position. Do not swim back from the handrail to your starting point— walk back.

Practice this for a long time. It is tiring, but keep it up because it is good exercise. When you really get exhausted, however, quit and relax for a while. But you should practice swimming this distance until it seems easy. *Only when you can swim 15 feet without difficulty, should you move on to step 5.*

STEP 5

Holding onto the handrail (the dock or poolside), walk out to *waist-deep water.* Put some kind of large marker on the dock or

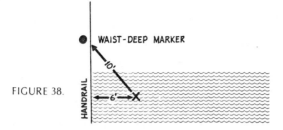

FIGURE 38.

poolside where it is waist deep. Or, if there is already some designating mark at that point, such as a painted number, use that as a marker. Go back into knee-deep water and look at the marker.

Find a starting point in knee-deep water that is about 6 feet from the handrail but 10 feet from your waist-deep marker (see figure 38). You are going to swim from that starting point in knee-deep water to the marker.

Now don't panic. It is true that you will be swimming at an angle into deeper water. And at some point along the course you won't be able to catch yourself by touching bottom with your hands. But try to put that out of your mind; *concentrate on the point you marked on the handrail.* You are going to swim to the handrail just the way you have been—just as though you were in entirely knee-deep water. You can do it.

Get into your prone position, facing the marker on the handrail. Remember, you are only swimming 10 feet. You are already able to swim 15 feet, so this is easy. Gather up your courage, swim to the marker and grasp the handrail. When you have done it once, walk back to your starting point in knee-deep water and do it again. Congratulate yourself that you are now able to swim in waist-deep water. You simply transferred the security of the arm-length bottom to the security of grasping the handrail. You're a success.

Continue to practice this exercise.

STEP 6

Move the starting point back to about 15 feet from the waist-deep marker (see figure 39). You can easily swim 15 feet—

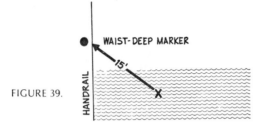

FIGURE 39.

you've done it many times in knee-deep water—so keep calm. Your starting point is still in knee-deep water, of course, so get into the prone position facing the marker. Again, gather your courage and swim to the marker. When you grasp the handrail, walk back to your starting point. Keep practicing this until you know you can do it any time you want to. You want to know you can do it even though you are afraid.

STEP 7

Holding onto the handrail, walk out into chest-deep water and place a marker on the dock or poolside at that point. Go back into knee-deep water and find a starting point about 15 feet from the marker. To do that you will need to move your starting point in knee-deep water closer to the handrail (see figure 40). When you establish your course, follow the same procedure: Get into the prone position in knee-deep water facing the marker, swim the crawl to the marker, grasp the

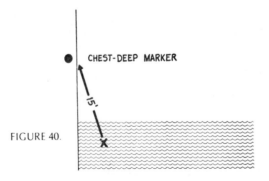

FIGURE 40.

handrail, and walk back to your starting point. Practice this many times, but *never do it when you are tired.* Rest between swims, and call it a day when you begin to feel exhausted. If your leg kicks and arm strokes get sloppy, that is a good warning sign that you are exhausted. So quit practicing immediately and go home.

STEP 8

You have now made an astounding achievement. You have gained enough confidence in your own swimming ability to challenge your fear and swim beyond the security of shallow water. Even though your fear constantly reminds you of your precarious position, concentration on the surface object has allowed you to battle that fear. You have by your own determination successfully transferred the need of touching bottom to the need of grasping the handrail. And that is the secret to deep-water swimming — to lose your dependence on shallow water.

For now we have substituted the handrail for the shallow water, but by the conclusion of this program you will have lost that dependence as well. You already have taken a very big step towards becoming a confident deepwater swimmer.

In later chapters we will have you swimming in water entirely over your head. For some, this will always remain a source of fear. To counteract that fear I will have you swim between surface objects such as rafts and docks, much in the same way that you are swimming now. For others, however, the fear of deep water will have almost disappeared by the time I ask you to swim in it. And that, of course, is my hope for you: I would like you to become a relaxed, confident swimmer — regardless of the water depth. But whether or not you ever do lose your fear of deep water, you will, for certain, gain sufficient confidence to challenge that fear on your own terms.

9
Back to Shallow Water: Getting You Familiar, Relaxed, and Floating

In the last chapter you were exposed to deeper water, and I hope the experience was successful for you. If you completed the lessons and swam despite your fear, the lessons were suc cessful, and you should be congratulated.

The time will come when you should practice swimming skills only in deeper water, leaving knee-deep water entirely. But for now let's return to the shallow water. You still must become more familiar with the water itself if you want to become a good swimmer. You must learn relaxation techniques and try to alleviate more of your fear. So let's practice these familiarity techniques in the most secure environment possible: let's go back to very shallow water.

Familiarity

STEP 1

After your experience in deeper water, knee-deep water should seem unusually comfortable. Practice your crawl stroke repeatedly, and see if you can improve your stroke and en- durance. Swim as far as you can. This is a good opportunity to test your skills, knowing that you only have to touch bottom with your hands to recover.

So far we have had you on top of the water only. Let's now try to get you into and under the water. You have made such good progress that I do not hesitate to suggest the following lessons.

STEP 2

If you have not been using the mask or goggles and noseplugs, get them now. You will be placing your head in the water, so wear the aids you think you need. Remember that the aids should be properly fitted. Make sure that they are tight but comfortable (see chapter 5).

Get into the prone position in knee-deep water and just relax. Keep your hands on the bottom and breathe normally through your mouth. Then take a breath, close your mouth, and place your face in the water. Do not submerge your whole head, just put your face into the surface water. If you are wearing a mask, put only the mask into the water first, and then gradually place your entire face in the water (see figure 41). Don't be afraid to open your eyes—no water will get into them. That's the purpose of the mask or goggles. Look around under the water for a brief moment, and then pull your face out of the water and breathe normally through your mouth. Not so bad, was it?

Continue to practice placing your face in the surface water. Practice holding your breath and looking around underwater. It is sort of pretty down there, you have to admit, especially if the water isn't too murky. Relax as much as possible. Don't let your

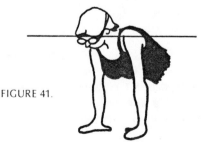

FIGURE 41.

"new" surroundings scare you. Remember that you cannot possibly sink. And no water can get into your eyes or nose if you are wearing a mask or goggles and noseplugs, so try to enjoy yourself. Practice holding your breath for a longer period of time so that you can extend your view of the underwater world. When you feel relaxed with your face in the water, proceed to step 3.

STEP 3

You should be in the prone position in knee-deep water, supported by your hands on the bottom. Now practice placing more of your head into the surface water. Lying there in the prone position, hold your breath, close your mouth, and gradually push your head further down until the water covers your ears (see figure 42). Try not to be afraid. Look around beneath the water and then pull your head out again. Continue to practice submerging half your head in the water.

FIGURE 42.

STEP 4

Now hold your breath and submerge your entire head into the water. Look at your hands; there is nothing to be afraid of. See how your hands are resting on the bottom. You cannot possibly sink. You have only to pull your head out of the water to take away your fear. Resist your fear and continue to practice submerging your entire head in the water (see figure 43).

FIGURE 43.

Practice this repeatedly until you can hold your breath and submerge your head without excessive fear. When you begin to feel confident in this exercise, proceed to step 5.

STEP 5

Now practice submerging your entire body (see figure 44). You should still be in the prone position in knee-deep water, with your hands on the bottom. Pretend you are doing push-ups. Hold your breath and gradually bend your elbows so that your entire head, shoulders, and back go underwater. Then push yourself back up into the prone position, pull your head out of the water, and breathe normally.

Go through this exercise again and again, but do it slower each time. Leave your eyes open all the while and look around. Try to stay completely submerged for five seconds before you push yourself back up. Gradually lengthen that time to ten seconds. Try to feel comfortable. Remember that you can push yourself up and out of the water anytime you wish. As you practice this exercise, relax as much as possible and try to enjoy yourself. When it finally does become enjoyable—even if that may means weeks of practice for you—proceed to "relaxation."

FIGURE 44.

Relaxation

You should be confident with the previous exercises. Now when you submerge your entire head and body, try to relax even more. Look forward and to both sides of you, not just down to the bottom. And look up too—see how the water surface looks from below. A pretty and unusual sight, isn't it?

Each time you come up for air, think of your next submergence as an adventure. Make a game out of it. Pretend, if you like, that you are skin diving in the Caribbean. Pick out pebbles or shells with one hand while the other hand keeps you balanced underwater. Then raise yourself to the surface and examine your find, and go back down and look for more.

If you would rather not rely on imagination ("Here I am diving near the barrier reef off St. Croix"), try throwing a marble or coin into the water and then going down after it. Or just submerge and enjoy the beauty of this shallow underwater world. If you are in a pool, you have the opportunity to see how various beautiful colors are formed as light becomes refracted in the water. The important thing is just to relax and enjoy the sensation of having water all around you. If the water is not too cold, the sensation of being entirely in water can be exhilarating.

Flotation

During these previous exercises in controlled submersion, you probably noticed that your body has a natural tendency to become buoyant. When you bent your elbows while in the prone position, and lowered your entire head, shoulders, and back into the water, it took very little arm muscle to keep your body from touching bottom. *Your body, in fact, resists sinking.* And if you relax enough, you will even find that it is not particularly difficult to float.

STEP 1

From the prone position in knee-deep water—with mask or goggles and noseplugs on and with hands secure on the bottom—hold your breath, close your mouth, and lower yourself again to complete submersion. Relax and check out the view. Now try to let your entire body come to rest on the bottom. You can do this by gradually bending your elbows more and more until your chest touches bottom. Leave your hands in position, however, so you can raise yourself up at any time you want to (see figure 45).

FIGURE 45.

If your chest actually does come to rest on the bottom, that's good. If your chest refuses to touch bottom, however, because it is too buoyant, that is even better. Keep practicing this exercise. Lower your entire body—from head to foot—as far down into the water as it will go. While you are down there look around through the mask or goggles and relax. It's really not so frightening, is it? When you run low on air, push with your arms as though you were doing a push-up, thereby raising yourself back up into the prone position again and surfacing above the water.

Repeat this exercise until you enjoy doing it.

STEP 2

You are by now very confident in shallow water. You are experienced in submerging yourself and raising yourself to the surface. Performing these maneuvers in knee-deep water is quite simple, and even enjoyable. So let's continue.

Get back into the prone position with your hands on the bottom. Hold your breath and practice submerging your entire body again. Let your head, shoulders, back, waist, and legs recline on or near the bottom. Keep your eyes open and look all around you. Relax and enjoy yourself. Your hands are still in place, so after a brief period of time do a push-up and rise to the surface and breathe normally. Very good.

Now let's do the same exercise with one variation: When you get down to the bottom, do not leave your hands in place. Instead, let your arms stretch out beside you. If your chest and stomach are resting on the bottom, you should have no problem removing your hands from their set position. Let your body support your weight as you make "wings" with your arms (see figure 46). If your chest and stomach are not resting on the bottom, release your hands from the bottom anyway, and make like a starfish. Spread your arms out like wings. You're floating! (See figure 47.)

To recover, simply place your hands on the bottom again and do a push-up. Do not be afraid—you are, after all, in very shallow water. And with your mask or goggles on, you should be

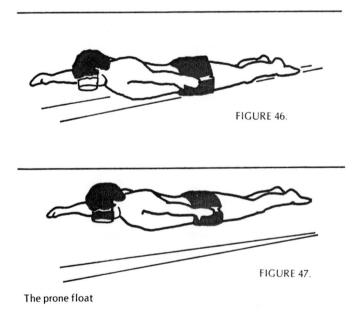

FIGURE 46.

FIGURE 47.

The prone float

able to see exactly what you are doing all the time you are underwater. So relax and experiment with this flotation technique. Practice it repeatedly.

STEP 3

You now have a basic understanding of the float, but as yet you may not be comfortable with the exercise or even with the idea of the exercise, so let's work on it some more. Here are some tips:

When you submerge, it makes little difference whether your body comes to rest on the bottom or whether it resists sinking. The important thing is to be able to submerge your body entirely into the water and let it go down as far as it will go. Because it is from this position that you begin to float—whether you know it or not.

When you release your hands from the bottom and spread them out into wings, you will begin to float. If your body has been resting on the bottom, it will tend to float up as you spread your arms. If your body refuses to touch bottom when you are totally submerged, floating will be that much easier for you. When you release your hands and make wings with your arms you will be floating!

As you begin to float, keep your head in a natural, relaxed position. Do not try to raise your head above the water surface. Let it lie horizontal like the rest of your body. Your eyes should, of course, be open, and you should be looking at the bottom as you float, getting some idea of how you are doing. When you get low on air, simply place your hands on the bottom and push yourself to the surface.

STEP 4

Keep practicing your float and try to loosen up. Relaxation is very important. Your floating technique may be technically perfect, but if you aren't relaxed you will not float properly. So work on your float until you feel at ease with it.

You should also know that flotation does not mean rising above the water surface. When you float you will rise to or near the surface, but that is all. *Do not be discouraged if you float beneath the surface of the water:* that is actually the normal floating position.

And don't worry yet about achieving a picture-perfect prone float. What is important now is that you relax and do some sort of prone float.

STEP 5

You should by this time be very comfortable with the prone float. So try now to perfect it. A good prone float is an essential skill for the remaining chapters. Here are a few more hints that should help:

When you inhale before submerging, take a deeper breath than you have been doing. Inflate your lungs so that your chest will serve as a buoy. Don't blow a gasket or anything, but take a hearty breath. You will find that you float higher in the water. Your back and shoulders will probably come to the surface.

Because of your lungs, your front half is more naturally buoyant than your rear half. You may have noticed that your legs even tend to sink when you're not moving them. So to facilitate a good prone float it is sometimes useful to kick slightly with your legs. Do not perform normal leg kicks. Instead, move your legs up and down in a very easy and casual motion. You will find that just the slightest kick will help keep your rear half buoyant (see figure 48).

Continue to work on your prone float. Practice it repeatedly. Get good at it. Enjoy your new skill and relax. By perfecting your prone float and increasing your sense of relaxation, you are taking a giant step toward becoming a good swimmer.

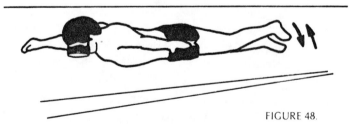

FIGURE 48.

Integrating What You've Learned

By the time you have reached the end of this chapter, you should be a relaxed floater in shallow water. As far as I am concerned, it is the most significant advance you have made yet.

Flotation is a very difficult exercise for fearful non-swimmers—as you well know. Too many instructors insist that pupils practice the float before any other exercise, and the result is that fearfuls freeze up, because they are simply not ready to float. So I introduced you to the idea of flotation in a very gradual manner. First you achieved water familiarity, and then you learned to become buoyant in shallow water by moving your arms and legs. You were even swimming—and swimming quite well, in fact—before you learned the prone float. Every swimming success increased your confidence in your own abilities and made you less tense in the water. Each time you progressed to a new lesson, you became more familiar with the water and a more relaxed swimmer. It was only then that you were introduced to the prone float, because without a sense of confidence and relaxation, a successful float is almost impossible.

The delay was necessary, but it was also necessary that you should learn to float, because *floating is an essential part of becoming a confident swimmer.* Before you learned to float, your swimming abilities were largely divorced from your knowledge of water. You were swimming, yes, but all the while you were swimming you understood very little about the water below you. Your fear constantly reminded you of your ignorance, and if it weren't for the shallowness of the water or the proximity of a surface object to grasp, you would have been in trouble. Teaching you to float and relax in the water, then, was a necessary lesson in understanding how water works, what it really is, and what you can do about it.

This was not just a lesson in the technique of flotation; it was another lesson in water familiarity. You learned how water looked from beneath the surface, what it felt like as it covered your entire body, and how simple it is to relax and enjoy the sensation of water. You came to understand some of the principles of water, and came to regard it less as your enemy and more as your friend. You finally learned to relax and let yourself become buoyant without moving your arms and legs—which is really what floating is.

You are now ready to become a good swimmer. You already possess swimming skills that give you enough confidence to challenge your fear and swim into waist- and chest-deep water. Now that you have learned to float and relax in the water, you are ready to integrate your previously learned skills with your newly acquired confidence. It is time for you to learn to swim in the same relaxed and knowledgeable manner in which you float.

10

From Floating to Swimming in Shallow Water

Swimming is the act of propelling yourself through the water while you float. If you can float, you can swim. And if you can already swim, the ability to float easily will make you an even better swimmer.

The Sustained Prone Float

Before you swim again, let's do some more work on your prone float. Our goal is for you to sustain your float for long periods of time. To accomplish that *you must learn to breathe while you float.* But don't worry. Achieving breath control while floating is not as impossible as it sounds, and it is a very important skill for future lessons.

STEP 1

When you performed the prone float in previous lessons, you practiced holding your breath while your head was submerged. After floating and holding your breath for a brief period of time, you recovered from the float by placing your hands on the bottom. Then you pushed yourself up, raised your head above the surface, and breathed normally through your mouth. That is basically the same procedure you should follow now to perform the sustained prone float. But instead of recovering from the float and then breathing, try now to breathe at intervals while you float. Here is how to do it:

Get into the prone position in knee-deep water, with your hands on the bottom for support. Let the water level touch the lower part of your chin. Breathe normally through your mouth. Now inhale through your mouth—just as though you were going to hold your breath—and place your head in the water. As your head lies in the water and you look through your mask or goggles at your hands, exhale slowly through your mouth. If you are not using noseplugs or a skin-diving mask, exhale slowly through both your mouth and nose. After exhaling most of the air from your lungs, close your mouth and gently raise your head forward and out of the water. When the water surface touches the bottom of your chin, open your mouth and inhale. *Never inhale through your nose.* Then when you have inhaled, again place your head under water and gradually exhale. Practice this breathing exercise again and again. Make this entire cycle of inhalation and exhalation as relaxed and natural as you possibly can. Practice this exercise until it becomes second nature to you (see figures 49–51).

Breath control for the sustained prone float should first be practiced with your hands on the bottom. Inhale through your mouth only. Exhale through your mouth or mouth and nose, depending upon the aids you are using.

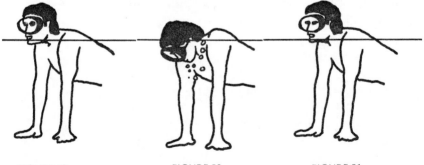

FIGURE 49.   FIGURE 50.   FIGURE 51.

STEP 2

Now, instead of holding your breath, let's try to integrate proper breath control into your prone float. Still in knee-deep water, perform a prone float. Relax and look through your mask or goggles at the underwater vistas below you. While you are floating in shallow water, slowly exhale the air you inhaled when you began the float. Then, when you complete exhaling and close your mouth, do not recover by placing your hands on the bottom. Instead, try to raise your head forward and out of the water *while* you float, exposing your mouth to the surface air. If your mouth *does* rise out of the water, open wide and *inhale.* Then, when you have inhaled, place your head back into its natural prone float position in the water and slowly exhale. The whole breathing cycle should be performed while you are floating. Recover by placing your hands on the bottom (see figures 52–54).

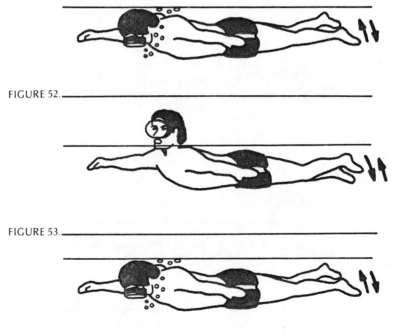

FIGURE 52.

FIGURE 53.

FIGURE 54.

The sustained prone float. Proper breath control for the sustained prone float is performed by raising the head *while floating.*

If your mouth does not rise above the waterline, do *not* inhale. Just return your head to its normal prone float position and relax. Then recover as usual by placing your hands on the bottom. You should be perfectly relaxed while you practice this exercise, but it is understandable if you aren't. You may be tense trying it for the first time, so you might not be performing your best float. Or, for that matter, you may not (for some purely physical reason) be the best floater in the world. In either case, this exercise will be easier for you if you take the following suggestion:

When you are about to raise your head forward while sustaining your prone float, think about your hands. Your arms should be spread like wings, and your hands should be palms down (see figure 55). *As you raise your head, simultaneously push the water down with your hands* (see figure 56). You will find that one quick downward push by both hands will enable you to raise your mouth above water. At that point, quickly *inhale* and return your head and arms to their normal prone float position. Relax and exhale slowly. Then recover by placing your hands on the bottom.

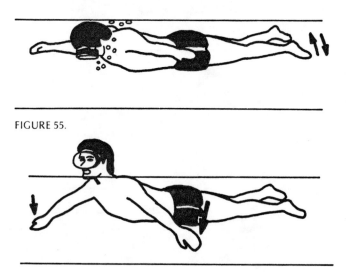

FIGURE 55.

FIGURE 56.

Proper breath control for the sustained prone float is often facilitated by a simultaneous downward push with both hands.

STEP 3

Rhythmic breathing is difficult to learn because to perform it correctly you must be relaxed, and it may be difficult for you to relax. Breathing rhythmically while you float may seem an awkward and risky business. Your head doesn't seem to move correctly, and water sometimes enters your mouth. But persevere. Take your time and make a conscious effort to stay calm. If water gets in your mouth after exhaling, spit it out just before you inhale. Or if you happen to swallow a mouthful while trying to inhale, don't panic. Gulp it down rather than trying to fight it, and then inhale again. Above all, remember that you are still in very shallow water. To recover and breathe normally you need only touch bottom with your hands.

Continue to practice this form of breath control while performing the prone float. Try to lengthen your time afloat. Instead of performing only one breathing cycle, try doing two or three breathing cycles before you recover by placing your hands on the bottom. And remember that a slight downward push with your hands will help you raise your head above the waterline. Just as a slight leg kick promotes a better prone float, so too will a slight downward push with both hands facilitate a better breathing cycle.

As you get more comfortable with this exercise, your head movement should become less jerky. Breath control should begin to seem like a natural part of your prone float. When you can sustain your prone float with proper breath control for five or six breathing cycles, you have mastered this exercise. Eventually you should be able to sustain your float indefinitely. But for now you have done well enough.

NOTE:

A word of caution: this is an important exercise, but for some of you it may be extremely difficult. If after much practice you honestly conclude that this is an exercise you just cannot perform, don't do it. Just skip this exercise whenever I suggest its use. Instead of breathing occasionally while you float, just hold your breath. If you can master this exercise, however, it will be much simpler for you to become a good swimmer. So keep practicing this exercise until you are fairly at ease with it. But if it gives you trouble, don't worry about it. The remaining lessons do not necessarily require that you be able to breathe while you float.

The Breaststroke
(from a Sustained Prone Float)

The breaststroke is similar to the dog paddle and is very easy to learn once you have mastered the sustained prone float. So I do not hesitate to introduce this new stroke into your learning program. Besides, it is a very relaxing swimming stroke, and one that promotes enjoyment of the water. But most important, the breaststroke represents an important transition in terms of proper breath control. It can be performed with the head kept entirely above water, but it is best performed in conjunction with rhythmic breathing.

Like it or not, rhythmic breathing is an important consideration in anyone's attempt to become a good swimmer. Although it is admittedly a difficult skill to acquire, once acquired it is very, very useful. If you have already learned to breathe rhythmically while you float, the breaststroke will now offer you the perfect opportunity to learn to breathe rhythmically while you swim.

STEP 1

The breaststroke is a variation of the dog paddle. The arm strokes are performed entirely *underwater*. Unlike the dog paddle or crawl, however, the arm stroke is not a forward-to-backward action. It is, instead, a *sideways* action. While the dog paddle and the crawl both push the water down and pull it back, the breaststroke pushes the water to the sides and leaves it there. And, unlike the dog paddle or crawl, the arms move *simultaneously* rather than alternately.

The entire arm stroke is illustrated in the following figures. From the prone float, both arms reach forward simultaneously until they are fully extended (figure 57). The hands are turned so the palms face out and away from each other, instead of down as in the crawl or dog paddle (figure 58). To begin the pulling stroke, the arms remain fully extended and both hands push sideways, thus pushing the water out and away from the body (figure 59). When both arms—still extended—point straight out from the body like wings, the head is raised out of the water (figure 60). Then both arms bend at the elbow, with the elbows pointing out from the sides (figure 61), and the hands move directly toward each other into the prayer position in front of the chest (figure 62). Just before they touch, the hands point forward and both arms reach until they are fully extended again

FIGURE 57.

FIGURE 58.

FIGURE 59.

FIGURE 60.

FIGURE 61.

FIGURE 62.

FIGURE 63.

FIGURE 64.

in the forward reaching position (figures 63 and 64). Then the hands rotate so that the palms face out and another sideways push begins.

Practice the entire arm stroke cycle out of water until you come to some understanding of how it works. Study the illustrations closely. Like the other strokes, it should be a smooth continuous movement of the arms.

The leg kick for the breaststroke is different than that of the dog paddle or crawl. But for now don't worry about it. Use your regular crawl leg kick. When you master the arm stroke, the leg action will come naturally, as you soon will discover.

STEP 2

When you think you understand how the arms and hands should function during the breaststroke, get back into knee-deep water and try it. From your prone float, extend your arms forward and go immediately into the breaststroke. Concentrate on pushing the water sideways with your hands. When you raise your head, keep it completely above the water and breathe normally. Do not put your head back into the water. Allow the sideways action of your arms and hands to propel you through the water and keep you buoyant. And don't forget to kick with your legs.

Your first attempts will be brief and probably a bit sloppy, but don't worry. Like any other swimming skill, a good breaststroke requires time and effort. As you practice, your breaststroke will improve, and you will gradually become more confident with it. Refer frequently to the illustrations and continue to practice. Eventually you will get a feel for how the breaststroke works. Done properly, it will keep you wonderfully buoyant (if you don't forget to kick). You will move smoothly through the water and will easily be able to keep your head above water while you practice. So breathe normally through your mouth and enjoy yourself.

STEP 3

If your leg kick begins to feel wrong, if it feels awkward and not the best possible movement in conjunction with your arm strokes — good! That means you are performing the arm strokes correctly. Now is the time for you to learn the proper leg kick for the breaststroke.

The leg kick is largely intuitive, but I can give you the basic idea of how it works. The leg kick should imitate the movement of a frog's legs: From a fully extended position, bend your legs at the knees so that your knees point almost sideways and the bottoms of your heels touch each other (see figure 65). Then, still keeping your heels together, bring your feet forward as far as possible. At this point your feet should be near your rump, and

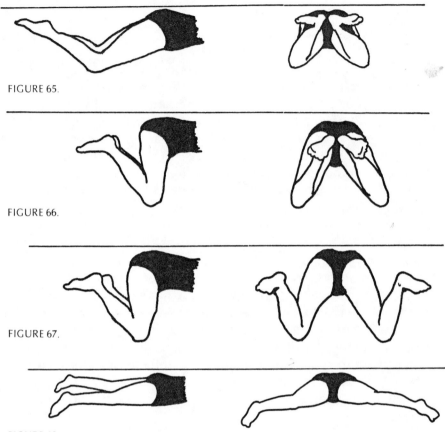

FIGURE 65.

FIGURE 66.

FIGURE 67.

FIGURE 68.

your knees, while still a little forward of your feet, should be down and away from your feet (see figure 66). From this tucked position, fully extend your legs into a spread position so that your legs form a wide V-shape (figures 67 and 68). The propelling action now begins. Instead of pushing the water down with your legs and feet as you do during the crawl or dog paddle, "squeeze" the water between your legs by bringing your legs together in one sudden powerful motion. When you thrust your legs together, you will "squeeze" the water *behind* you, thus forcing your body *forward* (figure 69). After thrusting your legs together, bend and separate your knees, bring your feet forward with heels touching, and begin another cycle (figure 70).

Practice this leg kick in conjunction with the proper arm stroke, and keep your head entirely above water. The trick is to

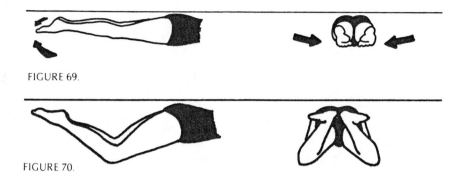

FIGURE 69.

FIGURE 70.

let the leg kick complement the arm stroke. The propelling actions of the arm strokes and leg kicks do not occur simultaneously. The arms push the water sideways while the legs tuck near the buttocks and then extend into a wide V-shape (see figure 71). Then the legs thrust together, forcing the water back, while the arms move toward each other into the prayer position and then reach forward in a fully extended position (see figure 72). In a sense, the arms and legs perform opposite actions even though they complement each other. While the arms propel you through the water by pushing out and sideways, the legs propel you by forcing themselves in and together. And even though the arm stroke and leg kick combine to make one smooth continuous motion, they are always in opposite positions. When the

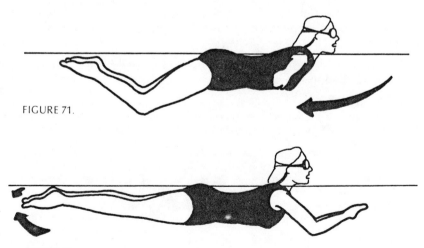

FIGURE 71.

FIGURE 72.

arms are spread out, the legs are together. When the legs are spread out, the arms are together. And when the arms are extended, the legs are tucked. When the legs are extended, the arms are bent.

STEP 4

Practice the proper arm stroke and leg kick until they both feel natural and efficient. That may take a while. But don't give up. You have plenty of time. So relax and enjoy yourself.

You should have no problem in keeping your head above water. As you practice, the movements of your arms should easily keep your front half buoyant, so breathe normally through your mouth. And remember that you are in very shallow water. When you want to rest, you need only place your hands on the bottom.

A suggestion or two may be helpful: As you get more experienced with the arm stroke, you should begin to restrict the movement of your hands and arms. The horizontal motion that you make with each hand should become smoother and less rigid. You should begin to make small horizontal circles with each hand. As you practice you should be able to visualize the two circular paths which lie in front of you (see figure 73).

And, as silly as it sounds, think of yourself as a frog. Try to remember what a frog looks like as he kicks his way across a lily pond on a languid summer evening. Then imitate that movement. Make exaggerated but relaxed motions, and glide through the water with each surge of power.

When you can perform the proper arm stroke and leg kick in a relaxed, synchronized manner, you will have mastered the breaststroke.

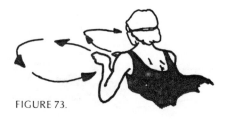

FIGURE 73.

STEP 5

Now we have only to integrate rhythmic breathing into your breaststroke and you will be on your way to complete success.

The easiest way to accomplish this is to perform a sustained prone float. Practice rhythmic breathing while you perform the prone float. Inhale and exhale in the manner described in the previous lesson. Remember to exhale through both your mouth and nose (if you are not wearing a nose aid). Some exhalation through the nose should prevent water from entering your nostrils. But *never inhale with your nose; inhale only through your mouth.* If you are wearing a nose aid, however, continue to inhale and exhale only through your mouth.

Now, as you practice rhythmic breathing while performing the sustained prone float, remember the old adage: If you can float, you can swim. And if you can breathe rhythmically while you float, you can breathe rhythmically while you swim.

When you inhale and put your head back into the water, instead of leaving your arms in their prone float position (wings), bring your arms forward and extend them in front of you into the reaching position. At the same time, bring your legs together (if they aren't already) and let them float straight behind you. You should be exhaling slowly while doing all this.

FIGURE 74.

Now with your hands pointed out and away from each other, begin the sideways stroke of your arms. Push the water to the side and away from you, as if you were clearing the water of debris. But keep your hands about 4 inches beneath the surface of the water.

FIGURE 75.

As your hands perform their sideways stroke and push the water away from you, raise your head forward and out of the water. Then *inhale* through your mouth. While you inhale, your legs should be bending at the knees and your feet should be moving forward toward your rump. Your arms should be completing their sideways push and then bending at the elbow.

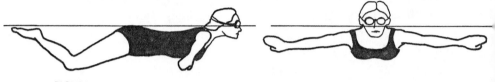

FIGURE 76.

Note that rhythmic breathing for the breaststroke and sustained prone float utilize the same head motion. The head rises forward and up out of the water. When the mouth is clear, the swimmer inhales.

FIGURE 77.

When you finish inhaling, place your head back into the water and move your hands down and toward each other into the prayer position. Your legs by this time should be in the wide V-shape, and you should be exhaling slowly through your mouth or mouth and nose.

FIGURE 78.

At this point, kick forcefully with your legs by quickly squeezing them together, thereby pushing the water backwards. And begin to reach forward with your arms.

FIGURE 79.

Bring your hands and arms forward into the outstretched reaching position and begin to bend your legs at the knees, all the while exhaling slowly. In this position you have completed one full cycle of the breaststroke. Then immediately begin another sideways stroke with your arms and hands, bringing your feet forward, and briefly raising your head to inhale again. Complete this second cycle just like the first, and then repeat for a third and fourth time. *Take one breath for each complete stroke cycle.*

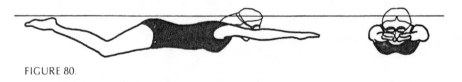

FIGURE 80.

STEP 6

Learning rhythmic breath control for the breaststroke is not simple. As with any other new skill, it may at first seem awkward and hazardous. But continue to practice until it begins to feel natural. Strive for fluid and continuous motion. Exhale while you swim, and then raise your head to *catch another breath without interrupting your breaststroke.* Try to relax as much as possible. If water should accidentally enter your mouth or nose, blow it out while you exhale or just before you inhale. Be brave. If you should gag or choke, don't panic. Go immediately to the head-above-water breaststroke. You should by now be able to perform an efficient head-above-water breaststroke, so catch your breath while you swim . . . or just recover by placing your hands on the bottom.

Repeat the breaststroke cycle after cycle until it becomes for you a natural coordination of arm stroke, leg kick, and rhythmic breath control. Don't rush yourself. Practice patiently until you can perform it correctly. When you finally do so, you will have become a good swimmer. You will be able to breathe rhythmically while you swim.

Back to the Crawl Stroke (from a Sustained Prone Float)

The crawl stroke is similar to the breaststroke in one respect: rhythmic breath control is not a necessary requirement. It is optional. You don't have to learn rhythmic breathing to be able to perform the crawl or the breaststroke. You can, if you wish, just leave your head above water while you swim. However, *if you want to learn to swim well, rhythmic breathing is necessary*. It is an essential part of becoming a skilled and confident swimmer. Both the breaststroke and the crawl are performed best if you utilize rhythmic breath control. So take a shot at it.

STEP 1

If you have completed the previous lesson and have (after much practice) a good grasp of the breaststroke, your progress is fantastic. You have become a relaxed swimmer in shallow water; you have learned that swimming is just moving yourself through the water while you float; and you have learned to breathe while you swim. You should be very proud of yourself.

We are now going to reintroduce the crawl. We want to improve your stroke and make you more confident with it. You are already familiar with the crawl and can perform it pretty well, so this lesson will focus primarily on rhythmic breathing and relaxation.

Begin by getting into the prone position in knee-deep water, with your hands on the bottom. Once again, perform a sustained prone float and begin to breathe rhythmically. You should be in a relaxed starfish-shape, with your arms spread out like wings, raising your head occasionally to inhale and then placing it back into the water to slowly exhale through your mouth (or mouth and nose) while you float.

STEP 2

Recover from the prone float simply by placing your hands on the bottom. Practice rhythmic breathing while you are in the prone position, only this time do it differently. Instead of raising your head up and forward to inhale, turn your head to the right side until your mouth is above the waterline. Then *inhale from the side instead of from the front.*

Let's go over that again in detail. Proper breath control for the crawl stroke incorporates an entirely new technique. You should look like the person in figures 81–83. Resting in the prone position with your hands on the bottom, place your head face down in the water, as though you were doing the prone float (see figure 81). When you want to inhale, instead of bringing your head straight forward and up as you do with the breaststroke, twist your head to the right until most of your face clears the water. Then, when your mouth is just barely above the waterline, inhale (see figure 82) and return your head to the face-down position. While in the face-down position, exhale slowly as though

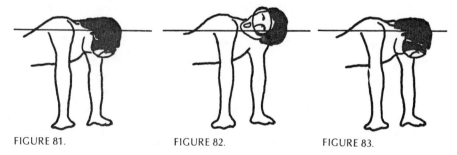

FIGURE 81.   FIGURE 82.   FIGURE 83.

Rhythmic breathing for the crawl stroke should first be practiced in the prone position with hands on the bottom. Unlike the breaststroke or sustained prone float, breath control for the crawl requires that you twist your head to the *side* to inhale.

you were performing a sustained prone float or breaststroke (see figure 83). (No matter which stroke you perform—the crawl or the breaststroke—you always exhale in the face-down position.) When you complete exhaling slowly, again twist your head to the right until your mouth is clear of the water and inhale, then return your head to the face-down position and exhale slowly again.

Repeat this cycle many times until it comes to feel natural. It should be a continuous smooth movement from the face-down exhaling position to the right-side inhaling position and back to the face-down position again. It should also be a relatively brief movement: inhaling should take no more time than necessary. Inhaling should be a very brief interval between the right and left motion of your head. And the entire movement of your head should take no more than three or four seconds. Exhalation, however, should take much longer. The head remains in the face-down position while you exhale slowly, and you *turn your head to inhale only when you have exhaled all your air.*

Take your time while you practice. Don't rush yourself. When you are totally confident with this form of breath control proceed to step 3.

STEP 3

We will now attempt to integrate this new breathing method into the crawl stroke itself. If you can successfully make the transition from our original head-above-water breathing method to this new rhythmic breathing method for the crawl stroke, you will automatically become an improved swimmer. So give it your best attempt. Work at it, if necessary, for months at a time. Integrating this new breathing method into your crawl stroke will make you a more relaxed and stronger swimmer. It will give you more stamina, allowing you to swim longer distances without getting as tired. It is definitely worth learning. So read the following instructions carefully, practice the movements on dry land, and then get back into the water and try it.

From your prone position in knee-deep water, with your hands on the bottom, take a deep breath and go into your prone float.

Then immediately begin to perform the crawl stroke, but leave your head in the water. *Do not raise your head above the surface as you did with your old crawl stroke.* Here is how to do it:

As you float, place your right arm in the forward reaching position—fully extending your entire arm in the surface water—and place your left arm in a backward position along your left side.

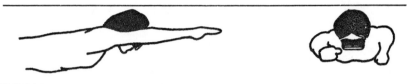

FIGURE 84.

Then begin a pulling stroke with your right arm: Pull the water down and straight back beside you with your right hand. When your right arm reaches a point approximately one-third the distance of the full-length stroke, activate your left arm: while your left arm is still trailing behind you, bend your elbow and bring first your arm and then your hand out of the water and begin to reach forward.

FIGURE 85.

As your right arm and hand reach the halfway point of the pulling stroke, your left arm should be entirely out of the water and beginning to point forward for the reaching stroke.

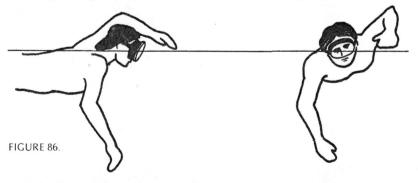

FIGURE 86.

When your left arm stretches into the reaching stroke, your right arm should be about two-thirds through its pulling stroke.

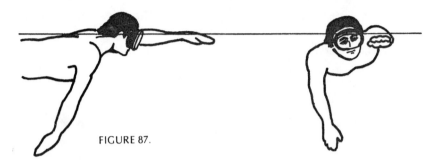

FIGURE 87.

Now, as your right arm completes its pulling stroke and your left arm begins its pulling stroke, casually (if possible) turn your head to the right and *inhale* when your mouth clears the water surface.

FIGURE 88.

As you inhale on your right side, your right arm should be completing its pulling stroke and beginning to lift out of the water. Your left arm should still be in the beginning stages of its pulling stroke.

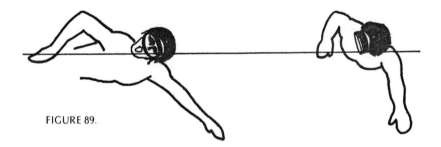

FIGURE 89.

When you complete inhaling and begin to turn your head back into the face-down position, your right arm should be entirely out of the water and beginning a forward motion, and your left arm should be powerfully pulling the water back at a point about one half the full-length stroke.

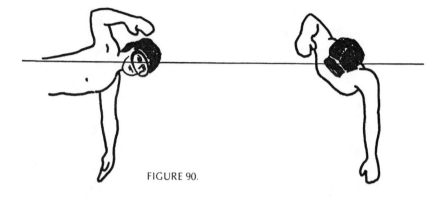

FIGURE 90.

As you continue to turn your head back into the face-down position and exhale slowly, your right arm should begin the reaching stroke and your left arm should be about two thirds through the pulling stroke.

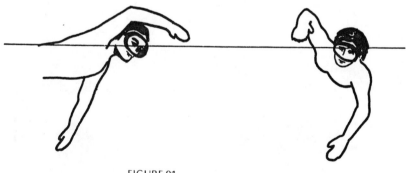

FIGURE 91.

When your head is completely back into the face-down position, your right arm should be completing its reaching stroke
and becoming fully extended in front of you; your left arm
should be about three quarters through the pulling stroke. At
this point you have completed one complete stroke cycle.

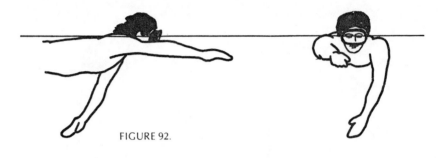

FIGURE 92.

You should then begin another pulling stroke with your right
arm: as your right arm pulls the water down and back to about
the one third point, and your left arm begins to come up and out
of the water, you should still be exhaling slowly in the face-
down position.

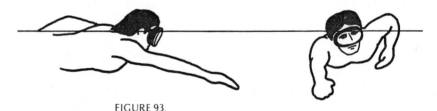

FIGURE 93.

When your left arm begins the reaching stroke, your right arm
should be approaching the halfway point of the pulling stroke.

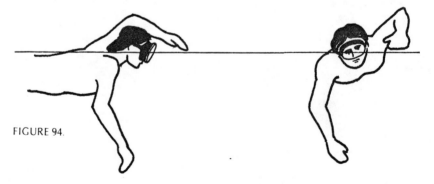

FIGURE 94.

As your left arm completes the reaching stroke, and your right arm completes the pulling stroke, you should then rotate your head to the right again and *inhale.*

FIGURE 95.

FIGURE 96.

When your right arm bends at the elbow and begins to come out of the water, and your left arm is pulling powerfully at approximately one third of the full pulling stroke, your head should be returning to its face-down position. At this point, exhale slowly and complete your second stroke cycle.

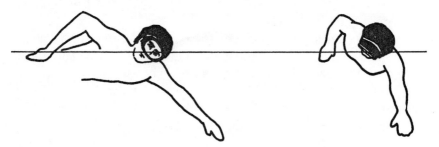

FIGURE 97.

If you should find that breathing from the left side rather than the right is more comfortable for you, by all means inhale from the left side. Follow the same procedure, but substitute the opposite arm. To get a visual representation of left side breathing, simply hold the illustration sequence up to a mirror.

NOTE:

Rhythmic breath control for the crawl stroke is a skill difficult to acquire. So don't be discouraged if you have problems at the beginning. It might take you a very long time to learn it, but you won't be alone. Many experienced swimmers—people who have been swimming for years—have never learned to breathe rhythmically while they crawl.

You can learn rhythmic breathing if you proceed slowly and use common sense. Don't rush yourself. If you encounter any problems—and you will—take them in stride. Don't let them bother you. Water in the nose or mouth is unpleasant, but you should know by now how to deal with it. Spit it out, blow it out, or gulp it down. If you should choke, go to your head-above-water crawl or breaststroke and catch your breath while you swim; or else just recover by placing your hands on the bottom Laugh it off or cry it off, but continue to practice.

STEP 4

You should, of course, be kicking your legs while you practice integrating rhythmic breathing with your crawl stroke. As complex as it seems, you do have to perform simultaneously all three aspects of the crawl: arm strokes, rhythmic breathing (to the side), and leg kicks.

The proper leg kick for the crawl, as you remember, is a scissors action and an alternately up-and-down motion. The idea is to push the water down with your entire leg and foot. As one leg pushes down, the other leg comes back up in anticipation of another downward kick.

Try as best you can to coordinate your arm strokes with our new breath control method. As you practice, replace jerky movements with more fluid movements. *The combination of arm strokes and rhythmic breathing should form one continuous and smooth motion.* And don't forget to do your leg kicks.

Performing the crawl in this manner may at first seem very difficult. There are many movements you must make at the same time, and I'll admit that it isn't easy. But with practice you will become more successful at it. Relearning the crawl in this way is almost like learning an entirely new swimming stroke, so be patient with yourself and practice diligently.

When you are somewhat confident with this integrated crawl, when you get it right some of the time, move on to step 5.

STEP 5

If you can perform our new integrated crawl with occasional success, you should now begin to coordinate the motion of your leg kicks with the motion of your arm strokes. This is necessary because your leg kicks are supposed to do more than keep your rear half buoyant; your leg kicks are supposed to work in harmony with your arm strokes so that your entire body participates in one fluid movement. Your leg kicks, in short, are supposed to balance and stabilize your arm strokes.

The best way to achieve this balance of arms and legs is to perform a six-beat crawl. The six-beat crawl, incidentally, looks more complicated on paper than it really is in practice.

THE SIX-BEAT CRAWL

As you swim, begin counting to yourself: one-two-three-four-five-six, one-two-three-four-five-six. Each full six-beat count should take about five seconds. And each series of beats should be regular and constant. At the count of *one,* extend your right arm in front of you and begin the pulling stroke. Simultaneously, kick down with your left leg. At the count of *two,* continue the pulling stroke with your right arm and begin to lift your left arm out of the water. Simultaneously, kick down with your right leg. At the count of *three,* your right arm should be about two thirds through its pulling stroke, and your left arm should be

The six-beat crawl:

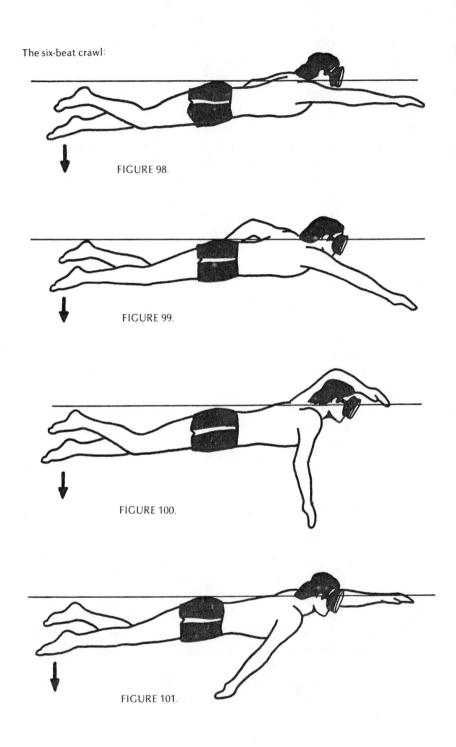

FIGURE 98.

FIGURE 99.

FIGURE 100.

FIGURE 101.

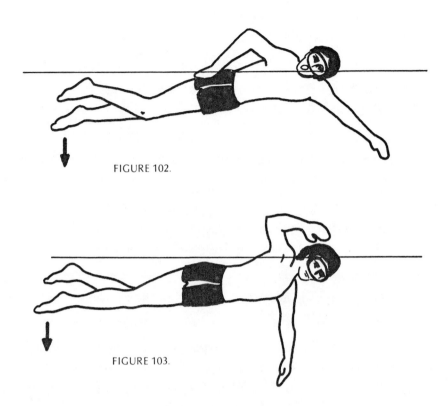

FIGURE 102.

FIGURE 103.

out of the water and reaching forward. Your left leg should now kick down. At the count of *four,* your left arm should be extended in front of you and beginning its pulling stroke. Your right arm should be completing its pulling stroke. And your right leg should now kick downward. At the count of *five,* your left arm should continue its pulling stroke and your right arm should begin to lift out of the water. Your left leg should now kick down. At the count of *six,* your left arm should be about two thirds through its pulling stroke, and your right arm should be out of the water and reaching forward. Your right leg should now kick down. Then, at the count of *one* again, your right arm is extended forward and begins another pulling stroke. Your left arm completes its pulling stroke, and your left leg kicks down. At this point you have completed one full six-beat cycle.

The trick is to keep calm and think. Your right arm begins its pulling stroke on the count of *one.* Your left arm begins its pull ing stroke on the count of *four. And each time either arm begins its pulling stroke, the opposite leg kicks down.*

Relax and stay within this six-beat system. Do not kick too hard or too fast. You don't need to kick frantically to stay atop the water. Such overkicking only leads to fatigue. Keep the leg kicks slow and deliberate. Think in terms of opposite balance: when your left arm begins its pulling stroke, kick with your right leg; when your right arm begins its pulling stroke, kick with your left leg.

You should know too that swimming coordination is largely intuitive. It doesn't need to be picture perfect to be effective. Like many other physical activities, you must learn by doing. I can show you how proper swimming coordination looks on paper, but it is you who must discover your own sense of coordination. The best coordination of arm strokes and leg kicks is the one you yourself develop as you practice the information given in this handbook.

You now have all the information necessary to learn a good crawl stroke. It is up to you to practice the crawl and to try to coordinate arm strokes, leg kicks, and rhythmic breath control.

The most important element in this entire lesson is your attitude. Be patient with yourself. Take your time, but work diligently. Above all, try to relax. A good swimmer is a relaxed swimmer. Remember that you are in very shallow water. Make slow, smooth, and deliberate movements with your arms, legs, and head, and you will become an efficient and strong swimmer.

11
Kickoff, Prone Glide, and Swim (in Shallow Water)

The integrated crawl is an optional lesson. Like the integrated breaststroke, it is not a necessary part of becoming a swimmer. It is, however, a necessary part of becoming a good swimmer. If the integrated crawl or the integrated breaststroke were not successful lessons for you, don't worry. We will still make you a swimmer, and a confident swimmer at that. But you should, as you improve in confidence and ability, return to those lessons and ultimately try to master them.

Even if you are still a head-above-water swimmer, you should by now have completed the relaxation and flotation techniques in chapter 9. And you should by now be a more relaxed swimmer. If, however, you still have problems with flotation and relaxation, return to those lessons and continue to practice them. *You must learn to be a comfortable floater and swimmer in shallow water before you proceed beyond this point.* The lessons that follow are preparations for your return to deeper water.

STEP 1

While we are still in knee-deep water, let's practice kicking off from the side of the pool or from a piling on the dock. From this kickoff we will go into a prone glide, a prone float, and then the crawl. Here's how to do it:

Go over to the handrail that you have been using and check it out. This should be the same handrail you used when you swam to your waist-deep marker and chest-deep marker in chapter 8. If you have been using the poolside for your handrail, that's perfect. The side of the pool will be your kicking-off wall. If you have been practicing at the beach and your handrail has been a dock, look for a vertical piling, or a horizontal bar that is just below the waterline, and use that for your kicking-off wall.

STEP 2

Get into the prone position next to your kicking-off wall, hold your breath, and go into a prone float. Float perpendicular to the wall, remembering that you are going to kick off from it (see figure 104). While you float with your arms spread like wings, push the water forward with your hands so that you move backward (see figure 105). When your feet touch the wall, bend your knees and get into a tucked position (see figure 106). Then, with your legs tucked against the wall, bring both your arms forward and *kick off* (see figures 107 and 108). Keep your head in the face-down position, and just let your entire body glide through the surface water. This is called the *prone glide,* and it should look like figure 109.

Kickoff and prone glide:

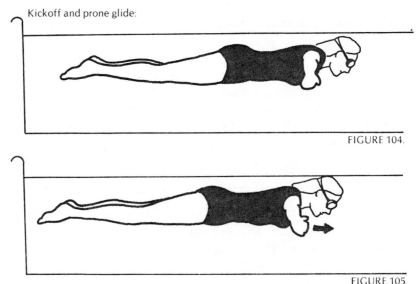

FIGURE 104.

FIGURE 105.

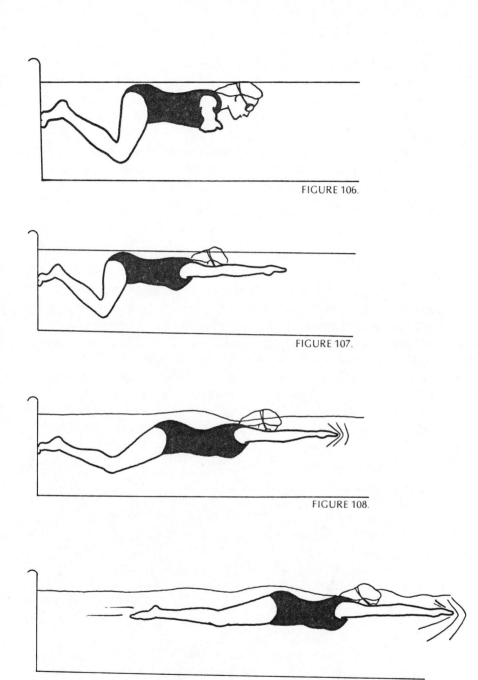

FIGURE 106.

FIGURE 107.

FIGURE 108.

FIGURE 109.

Prone gliding is a frolicsome exercise. It is a very pleasant sensation to fly through the water like a slippery dolphin. If you "fly" with your arms stretched out straight in front of you and your legs fully extended behind you, you are performing the prone glide correctly.

When the forward motion of your prone glide slows down, just place your hands on the bottom to recover, and go back to your kicking-off wall and practice again. Keep practicing the prone glide until it becomes a comfortable and delightful exercise.

STEP 3

You should by now be a skilled and happy prone glider in knee-deep water. Now, instead of recovering at the conclusion of the prone glide by placing your hands on the bottom, try going immediately into a sustained prone float. When your prone glide slows in its forward motion, simply let yourself remain buoyant by going into a prone float. Extend your arms to your sides and make wings, spread your legs out a bit, and breathe rhythmically. When you want to quit, simply place your hands on the bottom.

STEP 4

Now let's put rhythmic breath control into the entire exercise.

Just before you go into your prone float at the beginning of the exercise, take a deep breath—just as you have been doing. But instead of holding your breath as you float, *slowly exhale.* As you back toward the wall while you float, keep exhaling. And continue to exhale slowly as you tuck your legs against the wall, kick off, and prone glide through the water. Then, as the forward motion of your prone glide decreases, go into the sustained prone float. Raise your head forward until your mouth clears the water and *inhale.* The lower your head into the water again and exhale slowly. Sustain your prone float in this manner and breathe with ease. When you want to repeat the entire exercise, recover by placing your hands on the bottom and return to your kicking-off wall.

Practice this exercise repeatedly. The idea is to kick off from the wall, prone glide, and then perform a sustained prone float. This is a simple but valuable lesson. If you can do it well and with confidence, you are really making progress.

STEP 5

Now let's get you swimming from the kickoff and prone float.

When you kick off from the wall and go as usual from your prone glide into your sustained prone float, begin to think about the swimming strokes you have learned. As the forward motion of the prone glide slows, perform a sustained prone float and breathe rhythmically. Then begin to swim. Perform your breaststroke in either the rhythmic breathing form or the head-above-water form, and then go back into your sustained prone float. Then from your sustained prone float, perform your crawl. After you do the crawl for a while, again return to your sustained prone float. When you want to recover, simply place your hands on the bottom.

STEP 6

Keep practicing your newly acquired skills. And work on your endurance. Try to depend less on your hands-on-bottom method of recovery, and more on your sustained prone float method of recovery. Relax while you float, raising your head occasionally to inhale, and then swim again. Increase the length of your "sustained" swim. Swim-float-swim longer distances. If necessary, turn around occasionally and go back the other way. If you are swimming in a pool and are limited by its narrow width, put your new skills to good use. Turn yourself around while you perform a prone float and then kick off from the side of the pool. Or if you are at the beach, swim a sufficient distance and then just turn yourself around while you float and go immediately into the crawl or breaststroke and swim back the other way.

Remember to stay in very shallow water while you practice these exercises. If you tire, or for some other reason want to quit swimming and floating, all you need to do to recover is place your hands on the bottom. The ace in the hole is still there. But try not to use it. Pretend that you are in deeper water and cannot possibly touch bottom with your hands. Work diligently on the sustained swimming and floating method. It will make you a much better swimmer. Practice continually until you are confident with this new method of recovery. When, after much practice, you become confident with this method, you will be a very good swimmer, and one who is ready for deeper water again.

12
Back to
Deeper Water

When you first learned to swim in shallow water, you succeeded because the shallowness itself alleviated much of your fear. You knew you could depend on the security of the near bottom. Later, when I asked you to swim in deeper water, you succeeded because you learned to depend on surface objects for security. You were able to substitute ready surface objects for the accessibility of the near bottom. Now, after having become a sustained swimmer in shallow water, I want you to enter deeper water again and make still another transition. Instead of depending on surface objects for security, I want you to depend more on your own swimming abilities. You have already learned to sustain buoyancy by swimming and then floating and then swimming again. You have learned to depend on your own sustained float for security. Now I want you to take that well-learned and healthy dependence back into deeper water with you.

The transition from shallow water to deeper water will not be abrupt. Don't worry about that. We will reintroduce you gradually to deeper water, and with time you will perform as admirably in deeper water as you have in shallow water. It will be a painless transition, and very likely, a successful one. As before, we will be performing exercises that will slowly familiarize you with deeper water and your own abilities in it. But a large step towards a successful transition to deeper water will simply be your good attitude. You must convince yourself that you can perform the same skills in deeper water that you have performed successfully in shallow water. You have learned skills which eliminate the need of shallow water, and now you have only to convince yourself of that, and actually leave shallow water behind.

STEP 1

We'll begin with a familiar lesson. It's a good exercise to get you back into deeper water.

Place a marker on your handrail (dock or poolside) at a point where the water is about waist deep. Then go back into shallow (knee-deep) water and find a starting point about 15 feet from your marker.

Get into the prone position facing the marker, and perform a sustained prone float. Raise and lower your head in a graceful, relaxed manner as you breathe rhythmically. Once you are doing a good sustained float, begin to perform your integrated (rhythmic breathing) crawl stroke. If you have yet to master the integrated crawl, perform the head-above-water crawl. In either case, swim to the surface marker and grasp the handrail.

Repeat this exercise several times. When you are able to perform the entire exercise without any major difficulties, substitute the breaststroke for the crawl and practice again. Use rhythmic breathing, of course, if you can. Continue to practice until you feel comfortable swimming to your waist-deep marker.

Take your time, don't rush yourself. There is no hurry.

STEP 2

From your starting point in knee-deep water, assume the prone position and face your waist-deep surface marker. Perform a sustained prone float and then make the transition to the integrated crawl. If you cannot do an integrated crawl, do a head-above-water crawl instead. In either case, swim to the surface marker. This time, however, *when you approach the marker, do not grasp the handrail, but recover instead by performing a sustained prone float beside the handrail.*

If you become uneasy while sustaining the prone float, simply reach for the handrail. But try to relax when you do your sustained prone float. Breathe rhythmically and remain calm. Sustain your prone float for as long as possible. When you want to quit the prone float, reach for the handrail. If you have drifted away somewhat from the handrail, simply swim to it.

STEP 3

Let's continue to practice the sustained prone float in waist-deep water, and try to emphasize this form of recovery rather than the handrail method.

From your knee-deep-water starting point, swim out into waist-deep water to a point near, but not beside, the handrail. Let's say about 6 feet from the handrail. When you reach this point, sustain a prone float and relax. Breathe rhythmically and float as long as you like. When you want to quit, simply swim to the handrail.

If you don't like this idea, go back to step 2, and practice floating beside the handrail. When you gain confidence in your ability to recover by floating beside the handrail, return to this exercise (step 3) and practice your float recovery about 6 feet away from the handrail.

All this, of course, is meant to lessen your dependence on surface objects and to increase your confidence in recovering by means of the sustained prone float. This is an extremely important exercise. The sustained prone float recovery is one of the most useful swimming skills that you will ever learn. So practice step 2 and step 3 diligently. It will be well worth the effort.

When you feel at ease doing these exercises, proceed to the next step.

STEP 4

Now, instead of swimming into waist-deep water and then performing a sustained prone float, let's perform the sustained prone float from a standing position in waist-deep water.

Stand in waist-deep water beside the handrail, grasp the handrail with one hand, and begin to perform a prone float. As you become buoyant, release your hand from the handrail and relax.

While you are floating, begin rhythmic breathing and enjoy yourself. The view through your mask or goggles should be more interesting now that you are floating in waist-deep water. Look around and make a deliberate effort to relax. Sustain your prone float for as long as you like. When you want to quit, reach for the handrail.

STEP 5

This next exercise is the same as the last, with one exception. As you go into the prone float from a standing position in waist-deep water, do not grasp the handrail with one hand. Instead, just let yourself ease forward into the water. Extend your body and limbs into the prone float position and let yourself become buoyant. When you do become buoyant, begin rhythmic breathing and relax.

Remember that you are beside the handrail in waist-deep water. You're not going to sink. Any time you want to recover, just reach for the handrail. Give this exercise a fair try. Relax and let yourself become buoyant without the assistance of your hand on the handrail. Sustain your float as long as you can. When you want to quit, just reach for the handrail.

Repeat this exercise until you are comfortable with it. When you no longer hesitate, contemplate, and palpitate before each float, you are ready for the next lesson.

STEP 6

If you have mastered step 5, you are ready to swim from your waist-deep marker into shallow water and then back to the marker again.

Standing beside the handrail in waist-deep water, sustain a prone float without grasping the handrail. Just let yourself enter the water without any assistance. While you float, relax and breathe rhythmically. Strive for graceful motions as you raise your head occasionally to catch a breath. Now begin the crawl, swimming *toward the shallow water*. Do the integrated crawl if you can; otherwise do the head-above-water crawl. In either case, swim to the shallow water.

When you arrive in knee-deep water, do not recover by placing your hands on the bottom. Recover instead by sustaining a prone float. Breathe rhythmically. When you feel relaxed and rested—which is the idea behind any recovery—turn yourself around so that you face your waist-deep marker again. (The best way to do this is to raise your head above water and look around while turning yourself. The breaststroke is an excellent way to turn yourself—just push harder with one arm than with the other. (See figure 110.) When you get turned around so that you point in the direction of your waist-deep marker, swim back to the marker and grasp the handrail.

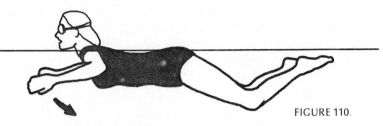

FIGURE 110.

The head-above-water breaststroke is a good way to turn yourself around while floating. Just push harder with one arm than with the other.

Repeat this exercise again and again. Remember how it works: From a standing position in waist-deep water, perform your sustained prone float. Then swim to shallow water and recover by sustaining another prone float. Do not touch bottom with your hands. When you are rested, turn yourself around by doing a modified breaststroke, and then swim back to the waist-deep marker and grasp the handrail.

Practice this exercise over and over. Take as much time as you want. It is important to get good at sustained swimming. You are making fine progress.

STEP 7

Place your marker at a point on the handrail where the water is chest deep. Having done that, repeat some of the same exercises you have just performed in waist-deep water. But perform them now in chest-deep water.

Standing in chest-deep water, beside the handrail, ease yourself forward into the water and perform a sustained prone float. Breathe rhythmically and relax. Chest-deep water isn't really any worse than waist-deep water, is it? Look around under water while you float, try to enjoy yourself.

If you would rather grasp the handrail with one hand as you ease into the prone float, go ahead. Just as in waist-deep water, a hand on the dock or poolside offers you more security, and it's all right to use that method at the beginning. But don't forget to release your grasp as you sustain your prone float. And when you become more confident in chest-deep water, be sure to practice without using your hand on the handrail. Just ease yourself into the water and perform a sustained prone float.

When you want to quit, simply reach for the handrail. Practice this exercise repeatedly so that you become quite comfortable floating in chest-deep water.

STEP 8

You are now going to swim from your marker in chest-deep water into shallow water and back to the marker again, all the while sustaining buoyancy.

You are ready for this, so don't panic.

From a standing position beside the handrail in chest-deep water, perform a sustained prone float. Do not use your hand on the rail for assistance. Breathe rhythmically and gracefully. Bring your head up occasionally to inhale, and then resume your head-down position to slowly exhale and relax. *You should be pointed towards the shallow water.*

Now begin to perform the crawl. Breathe rhythmically as you swim, if you have learned that technique, or else crawl with your head above the water. In either case, swim to the shallow water. When you arrive in knee-deep water, do not recover by placing your hands on the bottom. Recover instead by returning to a sustained prone float. When you have rested, turn yourself around (see step 6) so you face the marker, swim back to the chest-deep marker, and grasp the handrail.

If you should swallow some water as you swim to and from your chest-deep marker, stay calm. Do not try to touch bottom

or reach wildly for other people. *Rely on your swimming skills
for support.* Go immediately to your head-above-water breaststroke and recover your breath while you swim. Raise your head
and breathe normally as you perform a relaxed, easy breaststroke. Get to know and love your head-above-water breaststroke. It is a good way to recover from choking when you are in
deeper water (see figure 111).

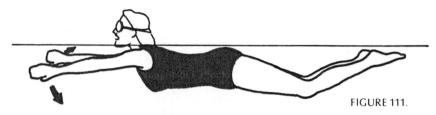

FIGURE 111.

The head-above-water breaststroke is a good way to catch your breath should you choke
while swimming.

STEP 9

Now perform the very same exercise, with one exception.
When you crawl stroke back to your position beside the handrail
in chest-deep water, do not grasp the handrail. Instead, recover
by sustaining a prone float. Breathe rhythmically and relax.

When you want to stop floating, simply reach for the handrail. If you have drifted away somewhat from the handrail as
you floated, don't panic. You are perfectly secure. Just begin
your crawl and swim to the handrail.

Practice this exercise repeatedly. Rely almost entirely upon
the sustained prone float for recovery. Breathe with ease while
you float. Continual practice will improve your endurance and
confidence in chest-deep water.

13
You Are Now a Confident Swimmer

You are now ready to swim between surface objects, and to eliminate shallow (knee-deep) water entirely. First you will swim between surface objects in waist-deep water, then you will swim between surface objects in chest-deep water. All the while you practice, you will not perform anything new. You have already learned all the skills necessary to complete this chapter. I will not ask you to do anything you haven't already done.

Eventually you will be able to swim with confidence between surface objects in much deeper water. For now, however, our goal is to improve your swimming strokes and your sense of relaxation. We want to work with the abilities you already possess, and by improving them, make you a self-assured swimmer.

STEP 1

Our first requirement is to find a better place to practice. For the lessons in this chapter, a swimming pool is strongly recommended. Pools possess everything we need: consistent depth changes, and two solid edges that can serve as surface objects. The sides of most pools run perfectly parallel and will be ideal as we practice first in waist-deep water and then in chest-deep water. So if you have been practicing until now at the beach, try to find a swimming pool to practice in. At this stage of your learning experience, it doesn't make much difference if the pool is crowded or not. You should be confident enough by now to handle even a very crowded public pool. Just make sure that the pool is no more than 25 feet wide, and not less than 15 feet wide. At the conclusion of this chapter, you can return to the beach. As a matter of fact, everyone will be going to the beach after this chapter.

If you have been practicing in a pool all this time, you're sitting pretty for now. But be ready soon to leave your cozy environment behind.

STEP 2

When you have found a swimming pool in which to practice, place your surface markers on both sides of the pool where the water is waist deep. You will be swimming across the width of the pool, not the length, so the depth of the water will be consistent (see figure 112).

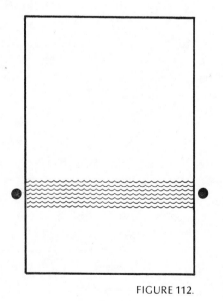

FIGURE 112.

If you are using a crowded public pool, or for some other reason don't want to be particularly obvious, you do not have to use the same markers you have been using. Towels make inconspicuous markers. You might also use some already established markers such as the poolside depth indicators—those saying "3 feet," for example—or benches, chairs, water-filter vents, ladders, etc. In any case, establish two markers—whatever they may be—on opposite sides of the pool where the water is waist-deep. You will be swimming between these two markers.

STEP 3

Okay, let's get into the pool and have some fun. Stand in waist-deep water beside one surface marker and look at your second marker. You are going to swim across the pool to the second marker and then swim back again. Here's how to do it:

Face the second marker and perform a sustained prone float. Do not use the hand-assist method. While you float, breathe rhythmically and relax. Then begin your crawl stroke and swim to the other side of the pool. Recover by grasping the handrail. When you have rested at the other side of the pool, swim back to the first marker using the same procedure. Sustain a prone float, then shift to your crawl stroke and swim to the handrail.

Repeat the exercise many times. Try to enjoy yourself.

STEP 4

Still in waist-deep water, continue to practice swimming between your two markers. If you have not yet mastered the integrated (rhythmic breathing) crawl this is a good opportunity to practice it. Go back to chapter 10 and review the techniques for the crawl with rhythmic breathing. Try to make a smooth transition from the sustained prone float to the integrated crawl. Stroke slowly and relax. When you reach the other side of the pool, recover by grasping the handrail.

Another way to refine your crawl stroke is simply to watch other people swim. Illustrations are very useful visual aids, of course, and you should study them carefully. But at some point it is more useful to see a stroke in action. So take an occasional break from your practice and observe good swimmers as they perform the crawl. Notice how they coordinate arm strokes, leg kicks, and rhythmic breath control and seem to make one fluid motion with the entire body. When you think you have the idea, get back into the water and try it.

STEP 5

Let's put some variety back into your practice sessions. Instead of shifting from your float to the crawl, kick off from the side of the pool and prone glide. When your prone glide slows down a bit, begin your crawl stroke. Here's how to do it:

Standing beside the edge of the pool, perform a sustained prone float. As you float, push yourself backwards by pushing the water forward with your hands. Continue to move backwards while you float until your feet touch the side of the pool. Then tuck your legs (knees bent down) against the side of the pool and kick off towards the other side. The thrust of your kickoff will enable you to prone glide at least half the width of the pool. When your prone glide slows, begin the crawl and swim to the other side. Recover by grasping the handrail (side of the pool).

Practice this exercise over and over. Swim between your two markers by floating, kicking off from the side, gliding, and practicing your crawl stroke.

STEP 6

Still in waist-deep water, continue the same exercise, only substitute the breaststroke for the crawl. Try to perfect the integrated breaststroke. Refer back to chapter 10 for the proper techniques. Even if you have become resigned to the head-above-water method, you might take this opportunity to try the integrated breaststroke again.

Then follow the same procedure as the previous exercise: float, kick off, prone glide, and then swim to the other side of the pool. Recover by grasping the handrail.

STEP 7

This is still the same exercise, but with another exception. When you reach the other side of the pool, instead of recovering by grasping the handrail, recover by sustaining a prone float. Breathe rhythmically as you sustain your float, and when you are rested, turn yourself around to point towards the first marker. Then kick off, prone glide, and swim back to it. This time recover by grasping the handrail.

Continue to practice this maneuver. From one side of the pool, prone float, kick off, prone glide, and breaststroke to the other side. When you reach the other side, recover with a sustained prone float, then turn yourself around and kick off, prone glide, and breaststroke back to the first side. Back at the first side, recover by grasping the handrail, and rest.

STEP 8

Continue to practice the same exercise, but now let's use a third method of recovery. Back at the first side, having completed two widths of the pool, recover without using your hands. When you feel the side of the pool, do not grasp the handrail, just stand up in the waist-deep water.

Until now your two most productive methods of recovery have been the handgrasp and the sustained prone float. But you should learn to recover in relatively shallow water by simply bringing your feet down to the bottom and standing up. As you become a more experienced swimmer, you may want to swim from a deepwater surface object into shallow water, and there will be no handrail available. For example, you may want to swim from a raft back to the beach. It is important, therefore, that you practice this simple method of recovery—the standing recovery. It is, you will find, a very natural way to complete a swim (see figures 113, 114, 115).

Practice the standing recovery until you are comfortable with it. At first you may be a bit hesitant, but remember that you are right beside the handrail. And the water is only waist deep. If you have any problems, you can simply reach for the handrail.

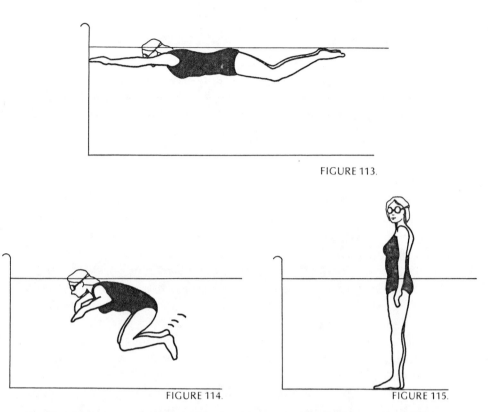

FIGURE 113.

FIGURE 114.

FIGURE 115.

The standing recovery. A good way to complete a swim in waist-deep or chest-deep water. Stabilize body movement with your arms while you drop your feet to the bottom. Then just stand up.

But I seriously doubt that you will find the standing recovery difficult. Just remember, for future reference, that the standing recovery is intended only for chest-deep or waist-deep water. It is, for rather obvious reasons, strictly a shallow water method of recovery.

STEP 9

Stay in waist-deep water and do the same exercise using the crawl stroke. From one side of the pool, prone float, kick off, prone glide and crawl to the other side. At the second side, recover by sustaining a prone float, then kick off, prone glide, and crawl back to the first side—where you should make a standing recovery—and congratulate yourself on a job well done.

Continue to practice and become more familiar with the standing recovery. When the entire exercise feels natural, proceed to the next step.

STEP 10

Let's revise the exercise a little. Instead of shifting to the crawl from a float, kickoff, and prone glide, go immediately into the prone glide and crawl from a standing position and then swim to the other side of the pool. To do this you must perform a standing pushoff.

Stand beside your first surface marker in waist-deep water and face across the width of the pool towards your second marker. Now, instead of performing a prone float and kicking off from the side of the pool, leap forward into the surface water by pushing off from the bottom. Then prone glide. Once in the prone glide, begin the crawl stroke as usual (see figures 116, 117, 118).

Remember, the standing pushoff is basically the same as the kickoff you have been performing from a prone float. The only difference is that now you can perform it from a standing position. Just lean forward, as you do when you begin a prone float in waist-deep water, and then push off from the bottom. The thrust of your pushoff should send you gliding through the surface water. As your prone glide slows, begin the crawl and swim to your marker. Recover by grasping the handrail.

Practice the standing pushoff until you can do it with ease. Leap forward and slide through the water. Feel the air bubbles as they rush past your ribs. Stretch yourself out and glide. It really is fun.

STEP 11

Okay. Let's put it all together.

Standing in waist-deep water beside your first marker, push off to a prone glide and then crawl to the other side of the pool.

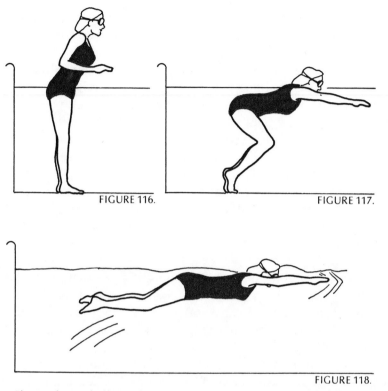

FIGURE 116.　　　　　　　　　　　FIGURE 117.

FIGURE 118.

The standing pushoff. Leap forward into the surface water and prone glide.

When you arrive at the second marker, do not grasp the handrail, but recover with a sustained prone float. When you feel like it, turn yourself around so you point back towards the first marker and kick off from the side of the pool. Do a prone glide and then crawl back to the first marker. When you reach the first marker again, make a standing recovery.

Practice this series of exercises repeatedly, and try to relax more and more each time. Make a special effort to improve your standing pushoff.

STEP 12

Let's now take these lessons into chest-deep water. Place your two markers at the sides of the pool where the water is chest-deep, and gather up your courage. There is no reason why you cannot perform these same exercises in chest-deep water, so let's get right to it.

Stand beside the first marker and go into a sustained prone float. You may use the hand-assist method, if you wish. Once in the prone float, breathe rhythmically and relax. Back yourself against the side of the pool and kick off toward the other side of the pool. When your prone glide slows, go into your crawl and swim the remaining distance. When you reach the other side, grasp the handrail to recover.

Repeat the same exercise back to the first side. Reacquaint yourself with chest-deep water.

STEP 13

This time, go directly into your prone glide from your standing pushoff in chest-deep water. Push off from the bottom and leap forward into the surface water. Go into your prone glide and then crawl to the other side of the pool. Recover by grasping the handrail.

Repeat the same exercise back to the first side marker. Then continue to practice swimming in this manner between the two sides.

STEP 14

Now try to relax more. When you reach the other side, recover by sustaining a prone float. Then, after you rest, turn yourself around so that you point back towards the first side, and kick off. From your kickoff go into your prone glide and crawl stroke. When you arrive back at the first side again, recover by grasping the handrail.

Practice this exercise repeatedly. Eventually replace the handrail recovery with a standing recovery. The whole exercise, then, should be performed as follows: From the first side in chest-deep water: standing pushoff, prone glide, crawl stroke, recovery by sustained prone float. From the second side: prone float, kickoff, prone glide, crawl, standing recovery.

When you master this exercise in chest-deep water, you will be a good swimmer!

STEP 15

Try to refine your strokes. If you are still unsure of the integrated crawl, refer back to chapter 10, and keep practicing, but now of course in chest-deep water. If your integrated breaststroke needs work, insert that into step 14 and practice it.

Relax more as you practice. Let your prone glide last as long as possible before you begin your swimming strokes; make an honest attempt to enjoy the sensation of gliding through the water. And keep your swimming strokes slow and efficient. Remember that fast, frantic arm strokes and leg kicks are more exhausting and less efficient than slower, more deliberate movements.

Take this opportunity to experiment with various relaxation techniques. For example, practice going back to a prone float from a prone glide; when you kick off from either the side or bottom of the pool, let your forward motion slow to a halt, then float. Whenever you want, restart your crawl or breaststroke and continue your swim to the other side. Another thing you should do is practice this sustained float recovery while swimming: as you crawl across the pool's width, interrupt your crawl stroke and perform a sustained prone float; then return to your crawl and continue your swim to the other side.

Also practice standing recoveries in chest-deep water in the middle of the pool between your two markers. As you swim across the pool, stop your swimming strokes and recover by standing up. And practice standing pushoffs from the middle of the pool. When you have performed a standing recovery in the middle of the pool, continue your swim by performing a standing pushoff and returning to your crawl stroke or breaststroke.

The important thing now is to relax and work on all the exercises in chest-deep water. Mix them up, do the exercises in a different order, and have fun. *But be sure to work on your sustained prone float recovery in the middle of the pool.* It is a very important relaxation technique, and its value as a method of recovery is limitless. Remember also to practice standing recoveries and standing pushoffs in the middle of the pool. And practice sustained prone floats from a standing position in the middle of the pool between your markers; then swim to either side or simply recover again by standing up. In short, be innovative now that you can swim in chest-deep water. Practice everything you know, and have fun. Amuse yourself with your versatility.

Do not proceed to the next chapter until you are completely confident with all skills in chest-deep water.

14
Deepwater Swimming

If you have progressed to this chapter, you have mastered basic swimming techniques in waist-deep and chest-deep water. It is now time to take those skills into still deeper water—water that is entirely over your head. But before we leave the pool and go to the beach, let's practice some preliminary deepwater swimming techniques within the familiarity of our pool.

Some amount of caution, however, is suggested. In this chapter you will for the first time be swimming in water that is over your head. You have the necessary skills to do so, and you should encounter no problems. *If you can swim in chest-deep water, you can swim in deep water.* Nonetheless, you should for safety's sake have someone watch you as you practice all the lessons in this chapter. Ask the lifeguard or another experienced swimmer to observe you as you practice. By doing so you are not admitting any sort of inadequacy. On the contrary, you are taking a reasonable and mature precaution against fear.

Above all, remember that *you will be performing the same exercises you have already mastered in waist-deep and chest-deep water.* That alone should give you confidence. We are only changing your environment, not your exercises. So be brave and have confidence in your already-proven abilities.

Still at the Pool

STEP 1

Leave your markers where they are. They should be along the two sides of the pool where the water is chest deep. You are now going to swim the length of the pool, as opposed to the width of the pool. Although your markers will no longer define your swimming course, they will serve as good reference points.

From a standing position near the side of the pool in waist-deep water, you are going to swim into deep water and grasp the handrail at the deep end of the pool. All the while you swim you will be within reaching distance of the side of the pool, so there is little to worry about. Here is how to do it:

Pretend there is an invisible line between your two chest-deep water markers. Stand in a position behind that invisible line, along one *side* of the pool in waist-deep water, facing the deep end of the pool (see figure 119). Perform a standing pushoff from

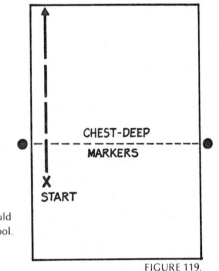

The first time you swim to the deep end of the pool, you should swim beside the edge of the pool.

FIGURE 119.

your position along the side of the pool, and go into your prone glide. From your prone glide go into your crawl stroke and swim to the deep end of the pool. Recover by grasping the handrail. Pull yourself out of the water, walk back to a point along the side of the pool where the water is waist deep, and get back into your starting position.

If this exercise was a frightening experience for you, don't worry. It should be. You just swam in water over your head for the first time. But keep practicing this exercise. Challenge your fear until it becomes less intense. Practice repeatedly. Remember to swim beside the edge of the pool. At no time should you stray beyond 3 feet from the side of the pool. If you have any problems, you need only reach for the side of the pool. But I doubt that you will have any problems.

If, perchance, this exercise was not particularly frightening for you, good! You may have already lost most of your fear of water.

When, after much practice, you feel somewhat comfortable with this exercise, proceed to the next step.

STEP 2

Repeat the previous exercise, only this time do not get out of the pool at the deep end. When you have recovered by grasping the handrail, turn around and face the shallow end of the pool while you hold onto the handrail. Now set the same course, only in reverse. Remember, you will still be swimming beside the edge of the pool.

Muster your courage, hold your breath, and perform a prone float as you release your grip on the handrail. Be sure to point towards the shallow end as you float. Now back yourself up against the end of the pool and kick off. From your kickoff go into your prone glide, and as your prone glide slows, begin your crawl stroke and swim back towards the shallow end of the pool. When you notice that you have passed beyond the invisible line between the two chest-deep markers and are again in waist-deep water, perform a standing recovery and congratulate yourself on a job well done (see figure 120).

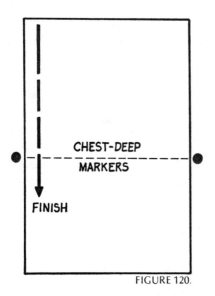

On your return from the deep end of the pool, do not stand up until you pass the chest-deep markers and are again in waist-deep water.

FIGURE 120.

Repeat this exercise many times. From your starting position along the side of the pool in waist-deep water, swim to the deep end of the pool and recover by grasping the handrail. Then prone float and kick off from the deep-end handrail, and swim back into waist-deep water, thereupon performing a standing recovery.

Continue to practice this two-part exercise until you feel more at ease in deep water. Take as much time as you need. That may mean weeks of practice, but fret not. There is no need to rush. You are doing just fine.

STEP 3

Let's practice all the skills we have learned and make the two-part exercise one smooth, continuous maneuver.

From your starting position along the side of the pool in waist-deep water, face the deep end and push off from the bottom. Sustain your prone glide as long as you can, then begin your crawl and swim the length of the pool. This time, however, do not grasp the deep-end handrail, but instead recover by performing a sustained prone float. When you have rested, turn yourself around while you float so that you point back towards the shallow end, and kick off. Then prone glide and begin your crawl stroke. Swim past the two markers back into the shallow end of the pool. When you return to waist-deep water, make a standing recovery. Once again, your entire swim should take place along the *side* of the pool (see figure 121).

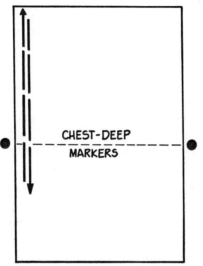

FIGURE 121.

If any aspect of this exercise frightens you, persevere! Keep doing it despite your fear. You do have the skills necessary to do these exercises in deep water, and you must continually remind yourself of that. So just confront your fear and deal with it. If, for example, you become nervous while performing a sustained prone float at the deep end of the pool, *don't panic.* But at the same time don't linger there too long. Turn yourself around, kick off, and get out of there. Then, as you repeat the exercise, take more time turning around at the deep end, until finally you are confident with your sustained prone float in deep water.

Do not proceed to the next lesson until you can perform this exercise with ease, whether it takes a week or a month. We're in no hurry.

STEP 4

If you are now confident with the previous exercises, move your starting point away from the side of the pool. No longer swim beside the edge of the pool. Instead, establish a starting position in waist-deep water which is in the middle of the pool. Then swim from your new starting position to the deep end of the pool and back to waist-deep water again. Here's how to do it:

Stand in the middle of the pool in waist-deep water and face the deep end. Push off from the bottom and go into your prone glide. Sustain your prone glide for a few seconds, and then begin your crawl stroke and swim to the deep end of the pool. As you near the deep-end handrail, sustain a prone float and breathe rhythmically. If you become tense, simply reach for the deep-end handrail. But try to control your tension. Try to relax as you sustain your prone float. When you are rested, turn yourself around so that you point toward the shallow end of the pool. Then kick off from the deep-end wall, prone glide, and begin your crawl stroke. When you swim past your two chest-deep markers, take a couple more strokes, and make a standing recovery.

Standing in waist-deep water you can pat yourself on the shoulder. You did it. You just swam the length of the pool without relying on the side of the pool. Congratulations!

STEP 5

Practice the previous lesson over and over again. Take your time. When you can perform all those skills while swimming the pool lengthwise, and can perform them with confidence, you will have made a tremendous achievement. You will have learned to swim in deep water. Perhaps you thought you never would!

We are about to go to the beach, and for some of you it will be a return engagement. But before we do, let's make full use of the pool. So far your experiences in deep water have been brief. You were only in deep water for short periods of time. Let's try increasing that length of time now, so that the beach won't come as a shock to you. There are only a few minor changes we need to make:

When you recover at the deep end by sustaining a prone float, be sure to do a legitimate sustained prone float. Don't rush into your kickoff, but float there for a while and breathe rhythmically. Make smooth, easy, graceful motions as you raise and lower your head. Then, when you are rested, turn yourself around and kick off.

When you become confident and comfortable with that exercise, you might also practice prone float recoveries while swimming in deep water. When you kick off from the deep end and go into your crawl from your prone glide, interrupt your crawl stroke over deep water and sustain a prone float. Then, when you have relaxed by floating, go back into your crawl stroke and continue your swim into the shallow end of the pool.

It is also a good idea to incorporate your breaststroke into these deep water exercises. Just substitute the breaststroke for the crawl stroke, and perform the exercises as usual.

NOTE:

These are all sophisticated exercises. Do not perform them unless you are ready for them. The idea is to increase your experience with deep water and at the same time to refine your swimming skills. But be safe. Do not push yourself beyond your limits. Relax as much as possible and practice intelligently. This is one of the most challenging parts of the entire course—and easily the most exciting. You are on the verge of becoming an excellent swimmer. Your confidence and your already learned abilities are directly challenging your fear of deep water. With a determined but reasoned effort you can defeat your fear and become a confident deepwater swimmer.

To the Beach

Until I introduced you to deepwater swimming, we had for the most part worked around your fears. But in this chapter we have found it necessary to challenge some of your fears outright. There is no other way for you to become a deepwater swimmer.

We didn't come to this decision unprepared, however. You previously learned all the skills necessary to become a deep-water swimmer. All you needed was courage and deter-mination—two ingredients you probably already possessed, or else you wouldn't have gotten this far.

Now it is time to put all your chips on the line. You are going to the beach to practice deepwater swimming. If you take all your skills and confidence with you, you will have no problems. And don't forget your skin-diving mask or goggles and noseplugs. You're still using those aids. Remember, I will not ask you to do anything you haven't already done. You are only changing your swimming environment.

You are ready to challenge your old nemesis—large bodies of water. *You do have the necessary skills to become a good deep-water swimmer.* So let's go!

STEP 1

The first thing you must do is locate an appropriate beach. Even if you had been using a beach previously, that one may no longer work. The beach you use from now on must fit your new learning needs. So if your old beach doesn't fit the following description, look around for another one that does.

Find a public beach that has two parallel docks that lead from the shore into deep water. The two docks should run perpendic-ular to the shoreline. (Many public beaches have parallel dock arrangements. Some of these parallel dock setups are disguised, however, so if you see any like those in figure 122, they will do

FIGURE 122.

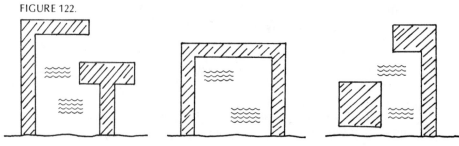

nicely.) The main requirement is that there not be too much distance between the docks. And the water should not be rough. You will be swimming *between* these two docks, so pick an area that is not too demanding. Remember the longest distance that you have swum previously, and try to find a beach that will provide you with that same distance. Don't try to swim beyond your limits.

When you pick your swimming area, check it out carefully before getting into the water. Determine the exact water depth at various locations beside the docks. If there are no depth indicators painted boldly on the docks, ask a lifeguard what the depth of the water is at various places. You will want to place a marker on *both docks* at a location where the water is chest deep. Those markers will divide the beach into deep and shallow halves. So remember that between the shoreline and the markers the water is shallow. Beyond the markers the water gets deep (see figure 123).

Once you have placed your chest-deep markers, you can then determine your various swimming courses.

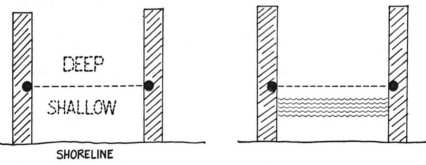

FIGURE 123.   FIGURE 124.

STEP 2

To begin, swim in waist-deep water. Your markers should now be positioned beside chest-deep water, so stay in the area behind your two markers, that is, in the area between your markers and the shoreline (see figure 124).

Standing anywhere in that waist-deep area, assume a sustained prone float from a standing position and then make a standing recovery. Repeat this exercise until you feel at ease in your new surroundings. Sustain your prone floats for thirty seconds or longer. Breathe rhythmically and with good form. Look around underwater while you float. Beach water isn't as clear as pool water, but don't let that frighten you. Obscurity is something we all encounter occasionally. When you want to recover, just stand up.

Now let's perform all the exercises we have learned. And if possible, let's swim from one dock to the other.

Standing beside one dock in waist-deep water, push off and go into your prone glide. Then begin your crawl stroke and swim towards the other dock. If your docks are more than 30 feet apart, you may tire before you reach the second one. If you become tired, just stop swimming and perform a standing recovery. Then continue your swim to the second dock by doing another standing pushoff, prone glide, and crawl stroke. When you reach it, recover by grasping the dock or just perform another standing recovery.

If possible, swim the entire length between the two docks. Take this opportunity to work on your endurance. Watch good swimmers. Notice how they swim with smooth, rhythmic motions and never seem to tire. If you can perform a proper integrated crawl, you too should be able to swim long distances without becoming exhausted. That is something you should work on.

Continue to practice swimming in the waist-deep area between the two docks. In addition to your sustained prone float, standing pushoff, prone glide, crawl stroke, and standing recovery, also practice your breaststroke and your sustained prone float recovery. As you swim from one dock to the other, mix these exercises up, perform them at random, and have a good time. Swim, then float, and then swim again. And stand up whenever you want to. Continue to practice these exercises until you are familiar with the beach.

STEP 3

Now let's go back into chest-deep water. That means that you will want to swim in the area directly between your two markers (see figure 125). As you swim between the markers in the chest-deep area, perform all the exercises. Here is a good example:

Standing beside your first marker, perform a standing pushoff and prone glide. Then begin your crawl stroke. After you swim a short distance, stop with a standing recovery. Then, when you are rested, perform a sustained prone float from a standing position. From your sustained float, begin your crawl stroke again and continue to swim to the other marker. When you reach the marker, recover by grasping the handrail (dock).

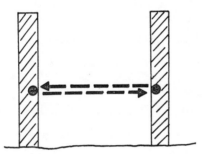

FIGURE 125.

Now standing beside the second dock and facing your first marker, do another sustained prone float. Then kick off and prone glide back towards your first marker. From the prone glide, shift to your breaststroke and swim about half the distance back to the first dock. Then stop swimming and make a sustained prone float recovery. Breathe rhythmically and with good form. When you are rested, continue your breaststroke and swim to the dock. Just before you reach the first marker again, perform another standing recovery.

Practice this series of exercises until you can do all the skills with ease. *If you should swallow water or choke as you practice, go immediately to your head-above-water breaststroke and catch your breath while you swim.* We all take in water at times; it's just something we must learn to deal with.

Become comfortable in chest-deep water at the beach. Get to know and enjoy your new surroundings.

STEP 4

Now let's swim in deep water again. You have proved in the pool that you can swim in deep water, so let's do it at the beach also.

Be sure to tell the lifeguard or other qualified observer where you will be swimming. The beach may be crowded and he or she will want to keep an eye on you.

Find a point on either one of your docks where the water is over your head. Place a third marker at that point. (If there is a ladder fixed to the dock in the area, use that as your third marker.) Now get back into chest-deep water and stand somewhere between your first two markers and face your third marker. You should position yourself no more than 25 feet from your third marker. If you have laid out this course correctly, you will be swimming in a diagonal direction (see figure 126).

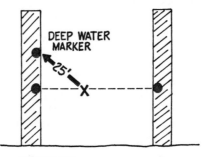

FIGURE 126.

Okay. From your starting position in chest-deep water, push off and prone glide in the direction of your third marker. Then begin your crawl stroke and swim to the marker. When you reach it, recover by grasping the handrail (dock or ladder). Then pull yourself out of the water onto the dock, or pull yourself along beside the dock back into chest-deep water.

Repeat this exercise over and over. Go back to your starting point in chest-deep water and swim to your deepwater marker. Then grasp the dock and return to your starting position. If this exercise scares you, confront your fear with common sense—this is nothing you haven't done previously. We have merely changed the environment. Instead of swimming to the deep end of the pool, you are swimming to a deepwater marker at the beach.

Practice until this exercise is not intimidating. Take as much time as necessary. That may mean weeks of practice. When you are comfortable with this exercise as well as the exercises in step 2 and step 3, proceed to the next step.

STEP 5

This lesson is basically the same as the previous one, except that now you will swim back from the deepwater marker to your starting position in chest-deep water.

When you recover by grasping the dock at the completion of your swim to the deepwater marker, remain in the water at that position. When you are rested from your swim, point yourself back towards shallow water so that you face your starting position in chest-deep water. Then perform a prone float, and if possible, kick off from the dock and prone glide. Begin your crawl stroke and swim back towards your chest-deep starting position. If there is not a good kickoff surface, just shift immediately to the crawl from your prone float. When you swim past your two chest-deep markers, stop swimming and make a standing recovery. That is very important. Do not stop swimming until you swim past your two chest-deep markers.

Continue to practice this entire exercise. Swim from your starting position in chest-deep water to your deep water marker, and then from your deepwater marker swim back past your chest-deep starting position. Try to relax more and more as you practice this exercise. When you can relax, and perform this entire exercise with confidence, keep practicing. But do not overwork yourself. Be very careful about that. When you feel exhausted, quit practicing for the day. You are on the verge of becoming a confident deepwater swimmer, and you have plenty of time. So take it easy.

STEP 6

If you have mastered the previous exercises, you are almost ready to swim between two deepwater surface objects. Before you do that, let's work on your endurance.

Standing beside your first chest-deep marker, swim the entire distance to your second chest-deep marker. Swim the full distance between the two docks. *Stay in chest-deep water.* Perform a standing pushoff and prone glide, and then go immediately into your crawl stroke. If at any time you tire, do not recover by standing up; instead recover by sustaining a prone float. Then when you are rested, begin your crawl stroke again and continue your swim to the second chest-deep marker. When you reach the marker, recover by grasping the dock.

Remember that the sustained prone float recovery is your single most important method of recovery for deepwater swimming. It is your ace in the hole. If you ever tire while swimming in deep water, or encounter any other problem, you can always float. You can rest your muscles and breathe without anxiety. There will be no need to panic. So become an accomplished sustained prone floater. Float for two or three minutes at a time, and r-e-l-a-x. This is a perfect time to practice. You are only in chest-deep water. *Swim, float, swim.* Sustain your swim for very long periods of time.

Practice continuously. Swim back and forth between your two chest-deep markers without touching bottom. Maintain total buoyancy for the entire distance between docks. Pretend you are in very deep water and cannot possibly touch bottom. Rely on your learned skills to swim the entire distance.

Take slow, efficient strokes when you perform the crawl. Make smooth, easy, graceful motions as you twist your head to the side to inhale and then return it to the face-down exhaling position. And relax as you swim. If you swim in an efficient and relaxed manner, you will have no problems developing your endurance.

Do not proceed to the next lesson until you are very confident swimming the entire distance between your two chest-deep markers.

STEP 7

You are now ready to swim between two deepwater surface objects, so read this lesson over carefully and then do it. Remember to tell the lifeguard where you will be swimming. He or she will probably want to keep a watchful eye on you.

Place a fourth marker directly across from your third marker so that you have two deepwater markers, just as you have two chest-deep markers. Together, the four markers should form a rectangle (see figure 127).

To begin, I want you to swim from chest-deep water to your first deepwater marker—just as you did in a previous lesson. Then swim between your two deepwater markers, and then back into chest-deep water again. Here's how to do it:

Locate a starting position in chest-deep water which is about 25 feet from your first deepwater marker. At this position in chest-deep water, face your first deepwater marker, do a standing pushoff, and prone glide. Then begin your crawl stroke and swim to the marker. When you reach it, recover by grasping the dock (see figure 128).

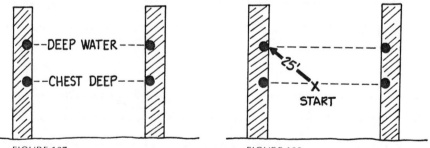

FIGURE 127.   FIGURE 128.

When you have rested, turn yourself around and face your second deepwater marker, and prepare yourself emotionally to swim the entire distance. You can swim the entire distance; you have already proved that. Now you must do it in deep water.

Facing your second deepwater marker, sustain a prone float. If there is something to kick off from, kick off, prone glide, and begin your crawl stroke. If there is nothing to kick off from, go directly into your crawl from your sustained prone float and swim toward your second deepwater marker (see figure 129). If your endurance is good enough to swim the entire distance, do so. However, if you become tired, recover by sustaining a prone float. Relax and breathe rhythmically. When rested, begin your crawl stroke again and continue your swim to your second deepwater marker. If you should happen to swallow water or choke at any time during the swim, do not panic. Go immediately to your head-above-water breaststroke and catch your breath while you swim. When you are breathing normally again, return to your integrated crawl and continue swimming to the second marker. When you reach the marker, recover by grasping the dock.

Having rested at your second deepwater marker, point yourself back toward chest-deep water and perform another sustained prone float. Then either kick off and prone glide, or shift directly to your crawl. Swim past the invisible line between your two chest-deep markers and make a standing recovery (see figure 130).

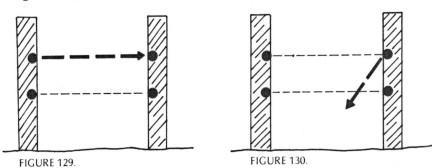

FIGURE 129.   FIGURE 130.

When you return to chest-deep water, you have completed one entire circuit of your course (see figure 131). And you have successfully swum between two surface objects in deep water. You are now a bona fide swimmer! You've done it!

Continue to practice this exercise until you feel less intimidated by deep water. But be careful not to overwork yourself on any given day. After a couple of laps, return to shallow water. And don't stray from your course! Until you are very confident in deep water, it is best to confine yourself to this particular

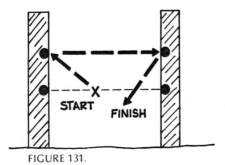

FIGURE 131.

layout: Swim from chest-deep water out to your first deepwater marker, from your first deepwater marker to your second deepwater marker, and then back to chest-deep water again.

STEP 8

Having proven to yourself that you can swim in deep water, vary your program a little. Spend more time in deep water. Practice swimming back and forth between your two deepwater markers. But *be careful not to tire yourself out.* At the first sign of exhaustion, quit practicing for the day, or else return to chest-deep or waist-deep water where it is safer to practice.

Try to relax more as you practice in deep water. Perform slow and efficient strokes as you crawl from one dock to the other. And practice the breaststroke. You should by now be able to perform both swimming strokes efficiently. So try to swim in deep water with the same confidence that you exhibit in chest-deep water.

But remember this one important rule: Confine your deep-water practices to exercises in confidence building. If you want to refine your swimming strokes, or if you want to try something new that you have heard or read about, practice in waist-deep or chest-deep water. *Never experiment in deep water.* Take only your already learned skills into deep water.

STEP 9

When you have become confident and comfortable swimming between your two deepwater markers, you have completed the final lesson offered in this handbook. Now design your own swimming courses based upon your own skills and ambitions. But *do not extend yourself beyond your limits in deep water.*

A good idea would be to participate in regular swimming activities. From waist-deep water, swim out to a nearby dock or raft in deep water and sunbathe for a while. Then get back into the water and prone float, kick off, prone glide, and swim back to the shallows.

If you want to increase your endurance so that you can swim longer distances, practice first in chest-deep water. Now that you can perform an excellent head-above-water breaststroke, you should be able to swim much longer distances. Swim the integrated crawl for a while, then do the head-above-water breaststroke—breathing easily and relaxing—and then return to your rhythmic breathing crawl. And don't forget your sustained prone float recovery. That is a very useful aid to long-distance swimming. An efficient swimming stroke, with rhythmic breath control, should, however, enable you to swim longer distances with little difficulty.

15
Conclusion

Still More to Learn

If you have performed all the lessons, you have completed the program. You can now swim limited distances safely, in either deep or shallow water. You should be proud of yourself. It took a lot of determination for you to become a swimmer, and you have succeeded.

Many of your recently acquired water skills, however, still need improvement. So continue to refine them. And there are other swimming skills—entirely new skills—that you should eventually learn to perform. You should, for example, learn to tread water, because treading water is a useful deepwater method of recovery. You should also learn to sidestroke, back float, and backstroke. And at some point you should take off your goggles and noseplugs or skin-diving mask and learn to swim without those aids. You should openly challenge your eye- and nose-related specific fears. However, this book cannot guide you through all the skills you should eventually learn. You will have to go the rest of the way on your own. But I can make some suggestions that should help you.

For those of you who are now very confident swimmers, I recommend that you enroll in a reputable conventional swimming class. The American Red Cross, for example, offers excellent courses in beginning, intermediate, and advanced swimming. Participation in such programs, now that you have already become a swimmer, will afford you a good opportunity to learn new skills and improve old ones. If you are not yet a very confident swimmer, and still don't fancy the idea of group instruction, I recommend that you continue to practice on your own. Get formal instruction from books or instructors or good swimmers you know personally, but wait to participate in formal training. Practice on your own in a familiar and secure environment. Take your time, and try to further your swimming abilities by yourself. When you do become very confident, then pursue formal training.

Where to Go from Here

How far you proceed as a swimmer depends largely upon your own ambitions. You may be content with the abilities you now possess. Since water is no longer your fierce enemy, you can participate in water activities much the same as anyone else. And with more individual practice you can improve your skills and become an even better, more relaxed swimmer. On the other hand, this course may have been only a beginning. Your learning experience here has revealed a sea of delights which you now can pursue. Water has become a new friend, and you want to become a complete swimmer. You want to go beyond the limited swimming instruction provided in this modest handbook, and I encourage you to do so. You should become the best swimmer that you can possibly be.

If, however, you have not yet successfully performed all the exercises in this handbook, keep practicing! Don't give up on yourself. Don't think that you are doomed to be a nonswimmer. When I created this handbook I did not expect everyone to meet with instant success. I realized that it would take different people different lengths of time to get into the water and become swimmers. I understood that for some fearfuls it would take a very long time to complete the course. But that is the beauty of this learning method. *You can take as long as you want.* And, as a matter of fact, you don't ever have to complete the entire course. So go back to the various exercises and practice at your own pace. Take a double dose of courage, work diligently, and keep the faith. Remember that the idea behind this handbook is to provide you with a basic source of information in your continuing effort to become a swimmer.

Good luck to you.

Index